Jon Hird

Miguel Ángel Almarza

Vincent A. Desmond

José Miguel Galarza

Peter Maggs

Pascual Pérez Paredes

Jenny Roden

Ruth Sánchez García

Nicholas Sheard

Russell Stannard

Piotrek Steinbrich

Inside Out

Resource
Pack

Advanced

MACMILLAN

Macmillan Education
Between Towns Road, Oxford OX4 3PP, UK
A division of Macmillan Publishers Limited
Companies and representatives throughout the world

ISBN 0 333 92345 6

First published 2001

Original design by Sarah Nicholson
Layout and composition by Red Giraffe
Illustrations by Red Giraffe
Cover design by Andrew Oliver

The authors and publishers would like to thank the following for
permission to reproduce their material:
Carlton Books Ltd for the 'Early Warning System' urban myth
from *The Best Book of Urban Myths Ever* by Yorick Brown and
Mike Flynn.

Whilst every effort has been made to locate the owners of
copyright, in some cases this has been unsuccessful. The
publishers apologise for any infringement or failure to
acknowledge the original sources and will be glad to
include any necessary correction in subsequent printings.

Printed and bound in Great Britain by Martins the Printers Ltd,
Berwick-upon-Tweed

2005 2004
10 9 8 7 6 5 4

Introduction

This Resource Pack for teachers contains thirty-seven practice activities for Advanced students of English. It is designed to be used with Inside Out Advanced Student's Book.

Eleven practising teachers have contributed activities, so you'll find a wealth of different ideas for practising skills and specific language points. All the activities have been tested in the classroom.

Using the worksheets

You can use the activities in many different ways. For example:
- to extend the lessons in the Student's Book
- as revision of points in the Student's Book, for example at the beginning of the following lesson
- to supplement other courses
- as a basis for standby lessons

How to use the Resource Pack

Each activity consists of one photocopiable worksheet original. The originals have been designed for maximum clarity when photocopied. However, if your photocopier has the facility to enlarge, you may sometimes find this useful – particularly for board games or worksheets which are to be cut up into cards.

Each original appears on the right-hand page, with teacher's notes on the left-hand page so that you can see them both at the same time. The notes explain the aims of the activity, describe the task, tell you what you need to do to prepare and then give a step by step lesson plan. This makes them easy to use if you haven't been teaching long, but it is also a terrific time-saver for experienced teachers. Regard the lesson plans as a starting point. As you use the worksheets you'll find your own ways of making the best of them in class. Some of the worksheets need cutting up into sections. To make these easier to handle in the classroom, glue them onto small pieces of card – index cards or blank business cards, available from most stationers, are ideal. After the lesson, file the cards in an envelope for the next time you use them. Write the name of the activity and the number of cards on the outside.

Some activities require multiple sets of cards. In these cases, it is a good idea to distinguish each set in some way. Put a different mark, preferably in different coloured pens, on the cards from each set. Or, even better, photocopy them on different coloured papers. This will save you time when you re-file them at the end of the lesson.

Over to you

If you have any comments about Inside Out, you will find a feedback form on our website at *www.insideout.net*, where you can also register to receive extra teaching materials free every week by e-mail. You opinions will help to shape our future publishing.

Contents

Worksheet	Timing	Task	Aim (lexis, grammar, pronunciation, skills)
8B *Cyber quiz*	20–30 minutes	To complete a quiz.	To review language related to the Internet. To discuss aspects of the Internet.
8C *Give us a clue*	30–40 minutes	To complete a crossword.	To practise defining words related to computers and the Internet.
9A *Thick as thieves*	30 minutes	To speculate about or deduce from the context the information which is missing from incomplete stories.	To practise speculating and making deductions.
9B *The suspect*	1–2 hours	To complete a dialogue.	To practise using fillers in conversation.
10A *Notable seconds*	30 minutes	To complete a general knowledge quiz.	To discuss answers to general knowledge questions.
10B *Beating about the bush*	20 minutes	To explain the meaning of expressions. To guess the expressions being described.	To practise expressions from Unit 10 of Inside Out Advanced Student's Book.
10C *The queue*	1–2 hours	To perform a one-act play.	To practise pronunciation, stress and intonation.
11A *Letters that changed history*	45 minutes	To write a letter.	To practise creative writing.
11B *Easy money*	30 minutes	To read and retell a story. To discuss reasons why a story could be true or false.	To practise reading for detail. To practise retelling a story.
11C *Compound adjective dominoes*	20 minutes	To match dominoes to make compound adjectives.	To practise forming compound adjectives.
12A *British and American English*	20–40 minutes	To complete a crossword with American English words.	To practise American English words.
12B *Ode to the spell checker*	20 minutes	To rewrite a poem with the correct spellings.	To identify homophones and correct the spellings.
12C *Word jigsaw*	40 minutes	To construct sentences containing words collected from a board game.	To revise vocabulary and grammar by constructing sentences.
13A *Pink dolphins*	60 minutes	To play a role in a discussion about ethical tourism and development.	To practise taking part in a meeting.
13B *Spare change*	1–2 hours	To perform a one-act play.	To practise pronunciation, stress and intonation.
14A *You bet!*	30–40 minutes	To correct the errors in fifteen sentences and to bet according to how confident the students are about their corrections.	To review and consolidate grammar and vocabulary from Units 8 to 13 of Inside Out Advanced Student's Book.
14B *Tell us about …*	30 minutes	To move around a board by speaking about different topics for sixty seconds at a time.	To improve fluency.
14C *Pair or pear?*	20 minutes	To match words to their definitions. To find words from their pronunciation and definition.	To practise homophones.

1A *Getting to know you*

Jon Hird

Type of activity

Speaking. Whole class.

Aim

To practise asking questions.

Task

To complete sentences about classmates by asking questions.

Preparation

Make one copy of the worksheet for each student.

Timing

30 minutes

Procedure

1   Give one copy of the worksheet to each student. Tell the students that they are going to find out more about each other and then complete the sentences with information about their classmates. Explain that they do this by mingling around the classroom, asking and answering appropriate questions to complete the sentences. For example,
What's your greatest achievement?
Which living person do you most admire?
What's your favourite journey? etc.
Students then write, for example,
Peter's greatest achievement is <u>overcoming his fear of spiders</u>.
The living person <u>Maria</u> most admires is <u>her grandmother</u>.
Lucy's favourite journey is <u>the walk upstairs at bedtime</u>.

2   Allow the students to move around the classroom talking to whomever they like, but encourage them to talk to as many different people as possible.

3   When the students have completed all the sentences, divide the class into pairs or small groups and ask them to share what they have found out about each other.

4   Conduct a class feedback session. Invite the students to report to the whole class anything interesting they have learned.

Follow up

Ask the students to write further questions to find out more about each other, and then interview each other.

1A *Getting to know you*

_____'s greatest achievement is _____

The living person _____ most admires is _____

_____'s favourite journey is _____

The best decision _____ has ever made was _____

The worst decision _____ has ever made was _____

_____'s most treasured possession is _____

The single best moment of _____'s life was _____

A word that sums up _____ is _____

One of _____'s negative characteristics is _____

The most amazing place _____ has ever visited is _____

_____'s idea of perfect happiness is _____

_____ is learning English because _____

The talent _____ would most like to have is _____

Something _____ really objects to is _____

A characteristic _____ really admires in people is _____

A characteristic _____ really dislikes in people is _____

_____'s greatest ambition is _____

_____ wishes he/she were more _____

1A *Getting to know you*

Photocopiable

1B *Bob the babysitter*

Miguel Ángel Almarza

Type of activity

Speaking. Group work.

Aim

To promote discussion on a controversial issue.

Task

To discuss and justify gender preferences for a variety of jobs.

Preparation

Make one copy of the worksheet for each student.

Timing

30 minutes

Procedure

1 Introduce the topic by asking the students if they think that there are jobs which are better suited to either men or women. For example, *Do women make better nurses? Do men make better doctors?*

2 Give each student a copy of the worksheet. Ask the students to look at the list of jobs and think about whether they have a preference for a man or a woman to do each job, and whether this preference is strong or mild, or if they have no preference. Allow students a few minutes to work through the jobs making their choices.

3 Divide the class into groups of four. (Try to have a mixture of male and female students in each group.) Explain that they are going to discuss their views and justify their reasons to the other members of the group. Encourage the students to be frank and really say what they think, even if it is not diplomatic or politically correct (since the point of the task is to promote discussion on a controversial issue). Point out the box of useful phrases at the bottom of the worksheet.

4 Before the students start the activity, do an example with the whole class. Make sure you are **not** politically correct to encourage discussion, for example,
If I were hiring a babysitter, I'd have a strong preference for a young woman. Women seem to have motherly feelings and are more sensitive and caring than men.
Ask one of the stronger students to agree or disagree with your beliefs.

5 After the discussion, ask each group to report their main points of agreement and disagreement to the class.

Follow up

Ask students to think of other jobs/skills or other aspects of society in which gender differences or stereotypes are prevalent.

Notes & comments

Monitor the group discussions and note down any arguments which are interesting, witty, etc. Introduce these arguments into other groups to raise more points for discussion.

1B *Bob the babysitter*

1   Do you have a preference (strong or mild) or no preference for a certain sex to do each of these jobs? Write *M* or *F* (male or female) and *S* or *M* (strong or mild), or NP (no preference) in each box.

	your dentist		your lawyer
	your babysitter		your hairdresser
	your child's primary teacher		your driving instructor
	your mechanic		your secretary
	your country's prime minister		your boss
	your bank manager		your fitness instructor
	the pilot of the plane you are in		your nurse
	your doctor		your teacher

2   In groups, discuss your views and explain your reasons.

Useful phrases

Men and women are equally capable of verb + *-ing* ...
Men/Women are better suited to verb + *-ing* because ...
Because of a personal experience, I believe that ...
I don't mind whether my _____ is male or female.
I'd rather my _____ was a man/woman because ...
If I had to choose between a man and a woman, I'd probably prefer ...

2A *Mineral or tap?*

José Miguel Galarza

Type of activity

Vocabulary. Group work.

Aim

To practise collocations with food and drink.

Task

To match dominoes to make collocations with food and drink.

Preparation

Make one copy of the worksheet for each group of three to four students. Cut up the dominoes as indicated.

Timing

20 minutes

Procedure

1 Explain that the students are going to play a game of dominoes in which they form types of food and drink. Elicit different ways food (e.g. meat, eggs) can be cooked and drinks (e.g. coffee, water) can be served.

2 Divide the class into groups of three to four students and give each group a set of dominoes placed face down on the table.

3 Ask the students to take five dominoes each and leave the rest in a pile, face down.

4 Ask the students to take turns to place their dominoes, for example,

potatoes | black · coffee | roast · potatoes | house

If they do not have a domino that works, they pick up a domino from the pile and miss a turn. Circulate, checking that the students have found the correct connections. The first student to get rid of all their dominoes wins. (Because of the crossover of different ways of cooking food, students may reach a stalemate situation towards the end where nobody can play. In this case, the student with the fewest dominoes wins.)

2A *Mineral or tap?*

potatoes	black	coffee	roast
potatoes	house	wine	fried
eggs	Caesar	salad	sparkling
wine	baked	fish	mineral
water	decaffeinated	coffee	potato
salad	fried	fish	red
wine	tap	water	fruit
salad	roast	beef	white
wine	hard-boiled	eggs	mashed
potatoes	steamed	fish	green
salad	sparkling	water	white
coffee	scrambled	eggs	baked

Photocopiable

2B *Restaurant reviews*

Miguel Ángel Almarza

Type of activity

Reading. Group work.

Aim

To practise scanning for information.

Task

To answer questions about restaurant reviews.

Preparation

Make three or four copies of the restaurant reviews section (enlarged if possible) and cut them up as indicated. Make one copy of the questions for each group of three to four students.

Timing

20 minutes

Procedure

1 Display a few copies of each of the six restaurant reviews around the classroom before setting the task.

2 Divide the class into groups of three to four students and give each group a copy of the questions. Explain that the questions are about the restaurant reviews which are displayed on the walls and that the students have five minutes to find the answers.

3 Ask the students to read the questions. Give them some time to decide within their groups on the most effective strategy for finding the twelve answers in the time given, for example, making different people responsible for different questions or each covering a different review.

4 Stop the activity after five minutes and check the answers with the whole class. The group with most correct answers wins.

5 Conduct a class feedback session. Ask students to comment on how effective their strategies were for finding the answers.

Answers

1 Brussels sprouts (Text 2)
2 catering (Text 3)
3 attracts customers by the truckload (Text 2)
4 top-notch (Text 6)
5 diners (Text 5)
6 The Stanville, Johannesburg (Text 1)
7 Chi Chi's, London (Text 5)
8 steak combo, mezedes, fajitas, canapes, guacamole, croquetas
9 Z Restaurant and Bar, Vienna (Text 3)
10 The Blue Olive, Madrid (Text 6)
11 The Blue Olive, Madrid (Text 6)
12 Foret des Amis, Paris; Lemonia, Crete

2B *Restaurant reviews*

1

The Stanville
Johannesburg

Located upstairs in a decrepit-looking building and gloomy and kitschy inside, but a big Jo'burg classic serving delicious South African curries.

Lunchtime only Mon–Sat.

2

Foret des Amis, Paris

This two-tiered bistro attracts customers by the truckload. Chef Richard prepares superb dishes such as veal chop with Brussels sprouts – so fresh and tasty that anyone would order an extra helping. With an excellent wine list and attentive service. Open 12.30–2.30 pm; 7.30–11 pm Tue–Sat.

3

VIENNA

RESTAURANT AND BAR

International cuisine from Austria's trendiest catering service. This central venue offers a popular but somewhat expensive lunchtime sushi-bar menu with weird and wonderful stir-fries for veggies. Seafood lovers should try king crab, and meat eaters the Uruguayan steak combo. Well-earned reputation for having the youngest and best-looking waiters in Vienna.

4

Lemonia, Crete

Good range of *mezede*s on offer, priced from 400 dr. The fish dishes, which include grilled octopus, calamari and tuna salad, are specially recommended. The place is always busy, so it's a good idea to get in early. Open Tue–Sun 12.00–3.00 pm; 8.00–12.00 pm.

5

Chi Chi's – London
This is the place for spicy Tex-Mex food and strong cocktails. On weekday lunchtimes you can eat as much as you like for only £5. This large restaurant operates on two floors, which allows diners to look down or out into the City whilst enjoying their tasty chillies and fajitas and bizarrely-named drinks. Sombreros get you in a south-of-the-border party mood.

6

The Blue Olive (Madrid)
A great stop-off if you're in the area. It offers the usual fare, but also some more unusual dishes such as chicken curry, mango and brie canapés and lovely, creamy guacamole. Great salads and top-notch croquetas. The resident DJ plays a good mix of laid-back sixties soul. Open daily, 1–4 pm and 8–1 am.

---

1 Which vegetable is mentioned?
2 What is the name for the industry which supplies food and drink?
3 Which expression (which includes a verb) means *lots of people come to this restaurant*?
4 Find an adjective which means *of the highest quality and standard*.
5 Find a noun which means the *customers in a restaurant*.
6 Which restaurant could do with a general refurbishment?
7 Where can you have a buffet lunch for a set price?
8 Name three non-English words for dishes.
9 Which restaurant serves Japanese food?
10 In which restaurant can you listen to music?
11 Which restaurant stays open the latest?
12 Which restaurants aren't open on Mondays?

Photocopiable

2C *A blind date*

Peter Maggs

Type of activity

Writing and speaking. Individual and group work.

Aim

To review past tenses.

Task

To create a story by completing sentences and inventing details.

Preparation

Make one copy of the worksheet for each student.

Timing

20 minutes

Procedure

1 Divide the class into groups of three to four students. Explain that they are going to write a story about going on a blind date.

2 Give one copy of the worksheet to each student. Give the students a few moments to look at the different stages. Then ask them to complete the first sentence. Encourage the students to be imaginative and amusing.

3 Ask the students to fold their worksheet back so that what they have written is hidden and the next unfinished sentence is visible. Ask them to pass their worksheet to the student on their left.

4 Ask the students to complete the sentence that is now at the top of the worksheet, fold their worksheet back and pass it to the student on their left as before. Repeat this until all the sentences have been completed.

5 When the last sentence has been written, ask the students to open out the completed story and read it to the others in their group.

6 Ask the students to choose the most interesting or amusing story in their group, which they then read to the whole class. The class listens to the stories and votes on the best.

2C *A blind date*

Complete one part of the story of a blind date. Then fold the paper over and pass it to the person on your left.

In preparation for my blind date last week, I had decided to wear ... (WHAT DID YOU WEAR?)

·· FOLD ··

As an ice-breaker, I had bought my date ... (WHAT HAD YOU BOUGHT?)

·· FOLD ··

We had arranged to meet in my favourite restaurant. (DESCRIBE IT)

·· FOLD ··

When I arrived, I couldn't believe my eyes. My date was wearing ... (WHAT WAS YOUR DATE WEARING?)

·· FOLD ··

After we had sat down, my date surprised me again by ordering ... (WHAT DID YOUR DATE ORDER?)

·· FOLD ··

Then, out of the blue, my date got up and ... (WHAT DID YOUR DATE DO?)

·· FOLD ··

Out of the corner of my eye, I noticed that the waiter was ... (WHAT WAS THE WAITER DOING?)

·· FOLD ··

Nobody could have anticipated what happened next but, as it turned out, it was the perfect end to the evening. (WHAT HAPPENED?)

3A *Olympic bid*

Vincent A. Desmond

Type of activity

Discussion and presentation to the class.
Group work.

Aims

To practise describing cities.
To practise emphasising.

Task

To prepare and present a bid to host the
Olympic Games.

Preparation

Make one copy of the worksheet for each student
and cut up the worksheet as indicated. Prepare
presentation materials as necessary (poster paper,
pens, etc.).

Timing

60–90 minutes

Procedure

1 Introduce the topic by asking the students to
   guess the answers to the following questions:
   a) How long do the Olympic Games last?
   b) How many athletes take part?
   c) How many officials run the Games?
   d) How many countries take part?
   e) How many media personnel attend?
   f) What is the world-wide audience?
   g) What is the total cost of running the
       Olympic Games?
   Answers: a) 16 days   b) 10,000
   c) 5,100   d) 200   e) 15,000
   f) 3.5 billion   g) over $2 billion

2 Give one copy of the Olympic Games Fact
   Sheet to each student and ask them to check
   their guesses.

3 Divide the class into groups of three to four
   students. Explain that each group is going to
   represent a city that would like to host the
   Olympic Games. Tell them they need to
   prepare a bid to promote the city. Allow the
   students a few minutes to choose their city.

4 Give each student a copy of the City
   Requirements part of the worksheet. Ask the
   groups to discuss these requirements in
   relation to their city, focussing on why their
   city is an attractive location, what facilities it
   has presently and what facilities they will
   have to develop/build for the Games.

5 Now ask the groups to prepare a ten-minute
   presentation. Provide any materials the
   students may require to make visual aids.
   Explain that each member of the group must
   speak during the presentation. Consider
   providing the groups with the following
   structure for their presentation:
   1   Introduction
   2   Location, climate and people of the city
   3   Sports facilities in the city
   4   Communications, accommodation and
       transport facilities
   5   Conclusion
   Provide students with useful phrases for
   emphasising (See Notes & comments).

6 Invite each group in turn to give their
   presentation to the class. Hold a class vote
   to choose which city wins the bid.

Notes & comments

Examples of emphasising from Inside Out
Advanced Student's Book are:
*You must realise **just** how exciting London is.*
*Tokyo is **actually** the most exciting city in the world.*
*New York **really** is the most exciting city in the world.*
***Never before** has a city like this hosted the Olympics.*
***Only in** a few other cities can you find these facilities.*
***Only after** considerable investment have we offered
our city.*
***Only by** visiting the city will you realise its beauty.*
***Not only** do we offer good transport links, but also
high levels of security.*
***Rarely** has such an opportunity presented itself.*

3A *Olympic bid*

Olympic Games Fact Sheet

The Olympic Games take place over sixteen days. During this time over 10,000 athletes and about 5,100 officials from 200 countries take part in 300 events in 28 different sports. These athletes, officials and spectators are joined by 15,000 media personnel providing various forms of coverage for a world-wide audience of 3.5 billion. So, with a total cost of over $2 billion, it is not surprising that the Olympic Games are backed by some of the world's leading financial and insurance companies as well as technology and systems sponsors. Providing the environment and resources for a successful Games takes planning and management. Making the Games special takes a special kind of magic. Can your city offer this?

 ....

City Requirements

Accommodation
- A modern stadium which can safely accommodate a crowd of 100,000 people
- Accommodation for 25,000 people who visit the city
- An Olympic village for 10,000 athletes and 5,000 staff must be provided near the stadium

Transport
- To and from the stadium (10,000 passengers per hour)
- For athletes, media and spectators to arrive at an airport and travel into the city

Security
- For the city and for the stadium

Press Facilities
- Full TV and communication facilities for about 5,000 media representatives

Environment and Multicultural Issues
- Policy for minimising pollution caused by the Games and protecting the natural environment (e.g. modern and innovative transportation)
- Policy for encouraging multicultural understanding, friendship and solidarity

Costs
- The city or regional/national government must agree to take responsibility for the cost of the Olympic Games

Photocopiable

3B *The Bronx*

Russell Stannard

Type of activity

Reading, speaking and writing. Group work.

Aims

To practise summarising a text.
To practise writing skills.

Tasks

To read and exchange information about
the Bronx.
To write an article for a guide book.

Preparation

Make one copy of the worksheet for each group of
four students. Cut up the worksheet as indicated.

Timing

40–50 minutes

Procedure

1   Introduce the topic by asking the students to
tell you anything they know about the Bronx,
for example, *Where is it? (New York City), What
is it like as an area? (considered by many to be
one of the worst areas in New York), Which
famous people are from the Bronx? (Calvin Klein,
Jennifer Lopez, Stanley Kubrick)*, etc.

2   Divide the class into groups of four students
and give each group a copy of the map. Give
each student in the group a different text
about the Bronx. Ask the students to read
their text and prepare to tell the rest of the
group about it. Circulate, helping with
vocabulary as necessary.

3   When they have finished, ask the students to
take turns to tell the rest of the group about
the text they read.

4   Then take the texts away from the students
and read out questions 1–8, one by one, for
the groups to answer. Check the answers with
the whole class.

5   Tell the students they are now going to write
an article about the Bronx for a guide book on
New York. Give the groups plenty of time to
plan their articles. Make sure everybody in
each group is involved in the planning and
writing stage. Circulate and monitor, helping
with vocabulary and ideas as necessary.

6   When the students have finished, display the
articles on the wall. Allow the groups time to
read each other's work.

Questions

1   What do you know about the death rate in
the Bronx area? (It is over 200 times higher
than in New York and some social groups
have lower life expectancies than countries
in the third world.)

2   Who starred in the film *Rumble in the
Bronx*? (Jackie Chan)

3   What was the story behind Robert De
Niro's film about the Bronx? (It is about a
young boy who becomes part of the Mafia
as a reward for not talking when he
witnessed a crime.)

4   What team has its home in the Bronx?
(New York Yankees)

5   What percentage of the population lives in
one-parent families headed by a female?
(Over 25 per cent)

6   What does EZ stand for? (Empowerment
Zone)

7   What percentage of residents within the
Bronx EZ area lives below the poverty line?
(42 per cent)

8   Which Bronxite famously defeated Sugar
Ray Robinson in 1943? (Jake La Motta)

Notes & comments

If the writing stage is done for homework,
encourage the students to find out more about the
Bronx using reference books and the Internet.

3B *The Bronx*

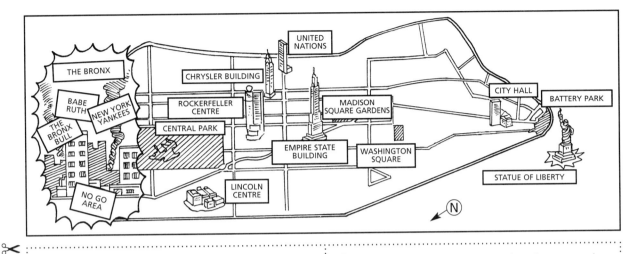

A The Bronx is considered to be one of the most dangerous areas in New York City and has one of the highest crime rates in the whole of the USA. The major effort has been to restrain the spread of slums, with their abandoned and burned-out buildings, closed-down stores and spreading crime. South Bronx is infested with drug addicts and pushers who lurk in abandoned buildings, the windows of which have been covered with metal and the doors of which are bricked up. Many areas within the Bronx are considered such no-go areas that the police often pick up straying tourists who accidentally go there after visiting Central Park.

B The image of the Bronx has been made even more infamous by a string of films based around the area. *Rumble in the Bronx*, starring Jackie Chan, is about a Hong Kong policeman who visits the area to attend his uncle's wedding but ends up fighting with the local Mafia and a local motorcycle gang. Robert De Niro's first film as a director is also set in the Bronx. *A Bronx Tale* deals with the problems of a young boy who witnesses a crime and refuses to speak to the police. The local Mafia rewards him by allowing him to become one of the group. Probably the most famous Bronx film is, however, *Raging Bull* starring Robert De Niro as an arrogant young boxer.

C Over one quarter of all families in the Bronx is headed by a single woman. The area has been designated an EZ area (Empowerment Zone entitled to special financial assistance from the Federal government). In 1990 the US census concluded that 42 per cent of the residents of the Bronx lived below the poverty line. Only 50 per cent of Bronxites are in employment which is 15 per cent less than the national average. The high crime rate combined with the levels of poverty mean that the death rate in the area is over 200 times that of New York City as a whole. Incredibly some social groups in the Bronx have life expectancy rates which compare with third world countries.

D The Bronx is home to the New York Yankees, the most successful baseball team in the USA. The team's nickname is the "Bronx Bombers". Several of the street names of the area are named after famous players, for example, Babe Ruth Plaza on 161st Street is named after Babe Ruth. Considered to be the best New York Yankee of all time, the "Babe" played in the 1920s, heading a batting line-up that was so good it was referred to as "Murderers' Row". Boxing also plays a major role in the Bronx. Jake La Motta grew up in a Bronx slum and turned to boxing while in jail. His first professional bout was in 1941, and on February 5th, 1943, he gained national recognition by handing Sugar Ray Robinson his first defeat. Nicknamed "The Bronx Bull" he lacked any great finesse and often allowed himself to take a severe beating before ferociously turning on his foe.

Photocopiable

4A *How do you say that?*

Ruth Sánchez García

Type of activity

Vocabulary. Pair work.

Aim

To practise verbs related to *talk*.

Task

To complete a crossword.

Preparation

Make one copy of the worksheet for each pair of students.

Timing

20 minutes

Procedure

1 Divide the class into pairs and give each pair a copy of the worksheet.

2 Tell the students that they are going to complete the crossword with verbs related to *talk*. Explain that the clues do not have numbers so the students have to work out from each clue what the verb is, write the verb in the correct place in the crossword and then write the crossword number in the box by the clue, e.g. *2D* for 2 Down, *3A* for 3 Across, etc.

3 Look at the first clue with the class. (The verb is *express* and the crossword number is 2D.) Make sure everybody understands.

4 In pairs, students complete the crossword and write the crossword numbers by the clues. Circulate, helping as necessary.

5 When most of the students have finished, check the answers with the whole class.

Answers

a	2D	express
b	12A	tell
c	5A	inform
d	11D	report
e	3D	muttering
f	8A	lectures
g	10A	interrupt
h	4A	chat
i	3A	mention
j	13A	explain
k	6D	dictated
l	4D	commented
m	7D	argue
n	1D	talk
o	9D	mumble

4A *How do you say that?*

Complete the clues and write the verbs in the correct place in the crossword. Then write the crossword number in the box, e.g. *1A* for 1 Across, *4D* for 4 Down, etc.

a   [*2D*]   He's very shy and it's very difficult for him to _e_ _x_ _p_ _r_ _e_ _s_ _s_ his feelings.

b   [   ]   He refused to _ _ _ _ me what happened.

c   [   ]   The manager wanted to _ _ _ _ _ _ us in person that the factory was going to close.

d   [   ]   I'm afraid I'll have to _ _ _ _ _ _ you to the headmaster.

e   [   ]   She walked off _ _ _ _ _ _ _ _ _ something under her breath about lazy workmen.

f   [   ]   She _ _ _ _ _ _ _ _ in history at the university.

g   [   ]   I hate it when you _ _ _ _ _ _ _ _ _ me when I'm speaking.

h   [   ]   I'll meet you after work for a coffee and we'll _ _ _ _ about it then.

i   [   ]   Oh, don't _ _ _ _ _ _ _ it, it's been a great pleasure to help you.

j   [   ]   If you don't understand, I'll _ _ _ _ _ _ _ it again.

k   [   ]   He _ _ _ _ _ _ _ _ the text slowly for the students to copy down in their notebooks.

l   [   ]   Nobody _ _ _ _ _ _ _ _ _ on Susan's bad behaviour.

m   [   ]   Don't _ _ _ _ _, Phillipa. Do as your mother says.

n   [   ]   Why won't you _ _ _ _ to me? Are you angry with me?

o   [   ]   Please don't _ _ _ _ _ _. Nobody can make out what you are saying.

Photocopiable

4B Over my dead body!

Piotrek Steinbrich

Type of activity

Speaking and writing. Pair work.

Aim

To practise expressions used in informal spoken language.

Task

To write a dialogue with expressions used in informal spoken language.

Preparation

Make one copy of the worksheet for each student. Provide monolingual dictionaries.

Timing

20–30 minutes

Procedure

1 Divide the class into pairs and give each student a copy of the worksheet. Explain that these are all common expressions used in spoken English and that they might not have seen them before.

2 Ask the students to read the expressions and try to work out what they mean. Then ask the pairs to compare their ideas with another pair. Encourage the students to use monolingual dictionaries to check their ideas.

3 Check the answers with the whole class. Encourage the students to think of situations in which the expressions could be used.

4 Ask the pairs to write a dialogue with some of the expressions from the worksheet. Circulate and monitor, helping with vocabulary and ideas as necessary.

5 Ask the students to act out their dialogues to the class. (If the class is too large for this, divide students into small groups.)

Answers

1 Cheers – for saying thank you

2 I'm easy – when you're given a choice and you don't mind which option is chosen

3 I can't be bothered – when you don't want to do something because you are feeling too lazy or you don't care

4 Please yourself – when you tell someone they can do what they like because you don't care

5 What are you getting at? – when you don't entirely understand the meaning behind what someone is saying to you

6 You bet! – when you are sure something will happen or that something is true

7 You can say what you like, but ... – when you are completely sure that you are right about something and you are not going to have your opinion changed

8 Be my guest – when somebody asks you for permission to do something and you are happy for them to do so

9 Over my dead body! – when you are determined to prevent something from happening

10 You can't have it both ways – when you tell someone they have to decide on one thing or the other

11 I'm all ears! – when you give someone your undivided attention

12 I'll take your word for it – when you accept that what someone is telling you is the truth

13 I wasn't born yesterday – used sarcastically when you want to make it clear that you think the other person is trying to mislead you

14 You could have fooled me – used sarcastically when someone tells you something and you believe the opposite to be true

15 That's more like it – when you tell somebody that something is more satisfactory than before

16 It's all go here – when it's extremely busy

17 There are no two ways about it – when you are emphasising that there is no doubt about a situation

18 You've been had! – when you tell someone they have been cheated

4B *Over my dead body!*

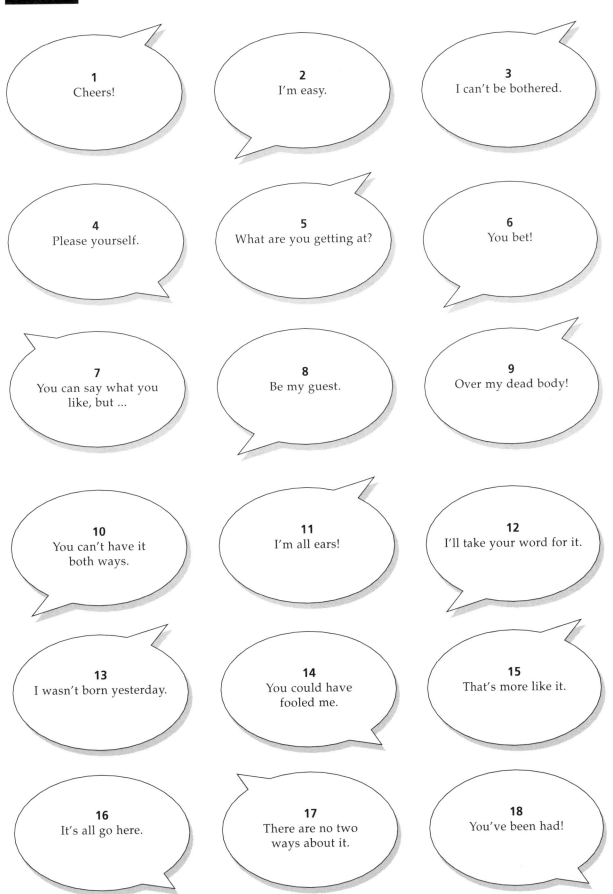

1
Cheers!

2
I'm easy.

3
I can't be bothered.

4
Please yourself.

5
What are you getting at?

6
You bet!

7
You can say what you like, but …

8
Be my guest.

9
Over my dead body!

10
You can't have it both ways.

11
I'm all ears!

12
I'll take your word for it.

13
I wasn't born yesterday.

14
You could have fooled me.

15
That's more like it.

16
It's all go here.

17
There are no two ways about it.

18
You've been had!

Photocopiable

4C *Hidden word*

Peter Maggs

Type of activity

Speaking and listening. Individual and group work.

Aim

To improve fluency.

Task

To speak for one minute, incorporating a designated word.

Preparation

Make one copy of the worksheet for each group of three to five students. Cut up the cards as indicated. Each group needs a watch with a second hand.

Timing

20 minutes

Procedure

1   Divide the class into groups of three to five students and give each group a set of cards placed face down on the table.

2   Explain that the students are going to take turns to pick up one of the cards (without showing it to the rest of the group) and speak for one minute on a topic. The topic is not what is written on the card but one chosen by the rest of the group, for example, the weather, shopping, British food, films, etc. The aim is to subtly include the word on the card in the speech. At the end of the minute, each student in the group guesses what the word was. If a student correctly guesses the word, he/she scores a point. If nobody guesses, the speaker scores the point. The student with the most points at the end of the game is the winner.

3   While the students are playing the game, circulate and monitor, noting down any errors which can be used for a correction activity at a later stage.

Follow up

Prepare a *Spot the mistake* or *Grammar auction* activity using the errors which you noted down while students were playing.

Notes & comments

This activity is based on an idea by Paul Jones. *Hidden word* can be used to recycle vocabulary that students have recently learned.

4C *Hidden word*

monkey	tennis racket	taxi driver	wedding ring
shop assistant	armchair	giraffe	passport
newspaper	London bus	trousers	spaghetti
umbrella	pilot	guitar	bicycle
dictionary	ice hockey	dolphin	chewing gum
cornflakes	bananas	ashtray	identity card
CD-ROM	The Beatles	footballer	underwear

Photocopiable

5A *Three wishes*

Vincent A. Desmond

Type of activity

Pyramid discussion. Speaking. Pair, group and class work.

Aim

To practise using hypothetical language.

Tasks

To think of three wishes to improve the world.
To reach a class consensus on the three best wishes.

Preparation

Make one copy of the worksheet for each pair of students. Cut up each worksheet into six cards.

Timing

30 minutes

Procedure

1   Introduce the topic of making wishes by drawing a genie on the board. Explain that the class has been granted three wishes by the genie which they are going to use to improve the world. Brainstorm a few example wishes with the class. ('Improving the world' is a wide topic: you can make it more specific, e.g. improving the city/town the students live in, improving the environment, improving the school, etc.)

2   Give each student three cards and give them a few minutes to decide on their three wishes.

3   Divide the class into pairs and ask each pair to reduce their combined total of six wishes to the best three. Encourage the students to explain why they chose these three wishes and what the benefits would be.

4   Combine the pairs into groups of four and ask them to repeat the activity, reducing the six wishes to the best three.

5   Continue combining the groups until the whole class has reached a consensus on the best three wishes.

5A *Three wishes*

I wish _____

_____

_____

I wish _____

_____

_____

I wish _____

_____

_____

I wish _____

_____

_____

I wish _____

_____

_____

I wish _____

_____

_____

Photocopiable

5B *Old wives' tales*

Russell Stannard

Type of activity

Reading. Pair work.

Aim

To talk about superstitions.

Task

To match two halves of a superstition.

Preparation

Make one copy of the worksheet for each pair of students. Cut up section B into cards as indicated.

Timing

30 minutes

Procedure

1 Ask the students if they know what *old wives' tales* are (superstitions). Encourage the students to tell you examples of old wives' tales from their countries.

2 Divide the class into pairs and give each pair section A of the worksheet. Explain that these are the first halves of some old wives' tales from Britain. Ask the students to read through them quickly and try to guess what the outcome of each situation is. Circulate, helping with vocabulary.

3 After a few minutes, give each pair a jumbled set of cards from section B of the worksheet. Ask the students to try to match the cards with the situations to complete the old wives' tales. Continue to circulate, helping with vocabulary.

4 Check the answers with the whole class. (The superstitious are correctly matched as they appear on the worksheet page.)

Follow up

For homework ask the students to write three more old wives' tales. Superstitions vary a lot from country to country and this often leads to a good mini-writing activity.

5B *Old wives' tales*

A	B
1 If you blow out all the candles on your birthday cake at the first puff,	you can make a wish and the wish will come true.
2 If you dream of fish,	it means someone you know is pregnant.
3 If your ear starts to itch,	it means that someone is talking about you.
4 If your hand starts to itch,	it means you're going to come into money in the near future.
5 If you break a mirror,	it will bring you seven years' bad luck.
6 If you sneeze, place a hand over your mouth	to stop your soul escaping.
7 Knock three times on wood after mentioning good fortune	so that evil spirits that hear you won't ruin it.
8 Put salt on the doorstep of a new house	to prevent any evil entering.
9 If someone is sweeping the floor and sweeps over your feet,	you'll never get married.
10 If a black cat walks towards you,	it brings good fortune.
11 If three people are photographed together,	the one in the middle will die first.
12 If you bite your tongue while you are talking,	it means you've been lying recently.
13 Open all the windows when someone dies	so that the soul can leave.
14 Keep a rabbit's foot in your pocket	to protect you from evil spirits.

Photocopiable

5C *Viv Nicholson*

Russell Stannard

Type of activity

Reading and speaking. Pair work.

Aim

To practise asking and answering questions.

Task

To exchange information to complete a text.

Preparation

Make one copy of the worksheet for each pair of students. Cut up the worksheet into sections A and B.

Timing

20 minutes

Procedure

1   Divide the class into pairs, A and B, and give each student the appropriate section of the worksheet. Tell the students not to show each other their texts.

2   Ask the students to read their text and write the questions they need to ask their partner to complete the gaps. Circulate and monitor, helping as necessary.

3   Then, working in pairs, students take it in turns to ask and answer the questions to complete their texts.

4   When they have finished, check the text with the whole class. Ask individual students to read out a sentence at a time.

Questions

1   What did Viv Nicholson and her husband become in 1961?

2   Where did they live at that time?

3   Where did they send their children?

4   In a TV interview, what did Viv famously promise to do?

5   How did her husband die?

6   What did she eventually spend all her money on?

7   What does Viv do today?

8   What kind of person is Viv?

---

a   How much did Viv and her husband win?

b   Who stopped talking to her?

c   How did they spend their time?

d   What was one of her favourite purchases?

e   How many times did Viv remarry?

f   What was she forced to become?

g   Why doesn't she bet or play the lottery anymore?

h   What does she know from experience?

Answers

1   the biggest pools' winners

2   on a council estate in Leeds

3   expensive boarding schools

4   spend, spend, spend

5   in a car crash

6   a constant stream of holidays

7   hairdresser

8   very cheerful and outgoing

a   £152,319

b   most of her neighbours

c   drinking, partying and shopping

d   an American Cadillac

e   three

f   dancer in a nightclub

g   it is against her religion

h   money doesn't bring happiness

Follow up

Tell the students to imagine that they have won £5 million and have a week to 'spend, spend, spend' it. Ask the students, working in groups, to plan what they would do with the money. Conduct a class feedback session to compare how everybody would spend the money.

5C *Viv Nicholson*

A

In 1961, Viv Nicholson and her husband became (1) _____ in history when they won £152,319 (about £7 million in today's terms). At that time, the couple lived (2) _____ in the north of England and had very little money. From that moment on everything changed for Viv and her family and friends.

Most of her neighbours stopped talking to her. The couple sent their children to (3) _____ and spent their time drinking, partying and shopping. In a TV interview at the time, Viv Nicholson famously promised to (4) "_____". And that is exactly what she did. One of her favourite purchases was an American Cadillac.

Over the next fifteen years, Viv Nicholson's life changed as dramatically as it had when she won the money. Her husband died (5) _____ and she remarried three more times. She travelled the world and eventually spent all her money on (6) _____. Eventually penniless, she was forced to become a dancer in a nightclub.

Today, Viv Nicholson is a Jehovah's Witness and she has returned to her hometown where she now works as a (7) _____. She doesn't bet or play the lottery anymore as it is against her religion.

Remarkably perhaps, Viv Nicholson is still a (8) _____ person. A person, however, who knows from experience that money doesn't bring happiness.

✂ ....

B

In 1961, Viv Nicholson and her husband became the biggest pools' winners in history when they won (a) _____ (about £7 million in today's terms). At that time, the couple lived on a council estate in Leeds in the north of England and had very little money. From that moment on everything changed for Viv and her family and friends.

(b) _____ stopped talking to her. The couple sent their children to expensive boarding schools and spent their time (c) _____. In a TV interview at the time, Viv Nicholson famously promised to "spend, spend, spend". And that is exactly what she did. One of her favourite purchases was (d) _____.

Over the next fifteen years, Viv Nicholson's life changed as dramatically as it had when she won the money. Her husband died in a car crash and she remarried (e) _____ more times. She travelled the world and eventually spent all her money on a constant stream of holidays. Eventually penniless, she was forced to become a (f) _____.

Today, Viv Nicholson is a Jehovah's Witness and she has returned to her hometown where she now works as a hairdresser. She doesn't bet or play the lottery anymore as (g) _____.

Remarkably perhaps, Viv Nicholson is still a very cheerful and outgoing person. A person, however, who knows from experience that (h) _____.

Photocopiable

6A *Memories*

Miguel Ángel Almarza

Type of activity

Speaking. Pair work.

Aim

To practise asking and answering questions.

Tasks

To answer questions about recent and distant memories.
To infer partner's questions by looking at his/her answers.

Preparation

Make a copy of the worksheet for each pair of students. Cut up the worksheet as indicated.

Timing

25 minutes

Procedure

1   Divide the class into pairs, A and B, and give each student the appropriate section of the worksheet. Tell the students not to show each other their worksheets.

2   Ask the students to read their questions and write brief answers.

3   When they have finished, ask the students to fold over their worksheets so that only their answers can be seen and then exchange worksheets with their partner.

4   Explain that the students have to look at their partner's answers and try to guess what the questions were. Their partner should not tell them the questions straight away if they are wrong but give clues to help them, for example,
Student A (reading the answer 'Chamonix, France'): *Is this your first holiday destination?*
Student B: *No, it isn't. But it's the place where I first saw something.*
Student A: *Is this where you first saw snow?*
Student B: *Yes, that's right.*

5   Encourage the students to ask questions to find out more information about some of the situations, for example, *Did you like it? What did you speak about?* etc.

6   Hold a class feedback session. Ask students to tell you which questions took them longer to answer than others. Invite some students to report to the class anything interesting they found out about their partner.

6A *Memories*

A

1 What was the last phone number you dialled? _____

2 What did you have for breakfast this morning? _____

3 How long did it take you to fall asleep last night? _____

4 What was your last conversation in English about? _____

5 What used to make you embarrassed as a teenager? _____

6 How did you celebrate your tenth birthday? _____

7 Where were you when you first saw snow? _____

8 What was your favourite TV programme as a child? _____

FOLD

B

1 Who was the first person you spoke to this morning? _____

2 What was the last item of clothing you bought? _____

3 What was the last book you read from start to finish? _____

4 When did you last go to the dentist? _____

5 What was your last argument about? _____

6 What was your first English teacher's name? _____

7 What was your favourite game as a child? _____

8 What used to make you frightened? _____

FOLD

6A *Memories*

Photocopiable

6B Mind the gap

Pascual Pérez Paredes

Type of activity

Reading and speaking. Individual and pair work.

Aim

To practise using words in which *mind* is a component.

Task

To complete newspaper extracts with words in which *mind* is a component.

Preparation

Make one copy of the worksheet for each student. Cut up the worksheet as indicated. Provide monolingual dictionaries.

Timing

20–30 minutes

Procedure

1 Explain to the students that the worksheet contains twelve newspaper extracts, each with a missing word, and they have to fill each gap with a word from the box. Tell the students that all the words contain the component *mind*.

2 Give a copy of the first part of the worksheet to each student and allow them time to read the excerpts and fill in the gaps, using monolingual dictionaries if necessary.

3 Ask the students to check their answers with a partner, then check the answers with the whole class.

4 Give pairs of students a copy of the questions part of the worksheet. Ask them to discuss the questions. Circulate and monitor, helping with ideas if necessary.

5 Conduct a class feedback session in which students report any interesting facts they found out about each other to the class.

Answers

1 masterminded
2 narrow-minded
3 mind-blowing
4 mind-numbing
5 mindful
6 mind-set
7 absent-minded
8 Community-minded
9 Business-minded
10 mindless
11 mind-boggling
12 single-minded

6B *Mind the gap*

1 Complete the gap in each newspaper extract with a word from the box.

> absent-minded   masterminded   mind-blowing   mind-boggling
> mind-numbing   mindful   mindless   mind-set   community-minded
> narrow-minded   single-minded   business-minded

The UN has demanded that the terrorists be handed over to the US to stand trial on charges that they (1) _____ last year's bombing of the embassy.

Several senior members of the Conservative Party were today described by the Liberal Party as (2) _____ bigots when they proposed ...

The basic plot of this latest in a series of sci-fi films wasn't particularly attention grabbing but the special effects were (3) _____. Most of the film's budget ($120m) was spent on the fight scenes with the Vardok aliens. The film's definitely worth seeing just for them.

Junior staff at the *Good Food* flagship supermarket in Essex were pleased to hear that robots would soon be doing all the (4) _____ jobs that were previously their responsibility. Special machines will soon be stacking shelves, doing stock checks and pricing items.

Motorists are asked to be (5) _____ of the poor road conditions this evening. Speeds of less than 50 mph on the motorway are recommended.

I don't think the relationship you describe has any chance of survival. The couple are of a different (6) _____. If your brother doesn't make the effort to understand why his wife has these views and attitudes, it will spell disaster for their marriage.

This long awaited biography of Einstein, the seemingly (7) '_____ professor', is bound to be a best-seller.

(8) _____ parents on the Island of Soay in the north of Scotland have fought to keep their local primary school open. With only six pupils, aged five to eight, the local school had been faced with closure and the children with being forced to attend another school a boat trip away.

(9) _____ teenagers are taking advantage of the anonymity of Internet trading, where age is an irrelevance, to become some of Britain's richest entrepreneurs.

Extra police have been brought in to man the streets of London after a series of (10) _____ acts of vandalism in and around Trafalgar Square.

The amount of money some high profile Hollywood actors are being paid has now reached (11) _____ proportions. The basic fee combined with a percentage of takings and merchandising can now earn some actors in the region of $40 million per film.

Ellen's (12) _____ determination to succeed earned her second place. With this amazing feat she has earned her place in history as the youngest and fastest woman to sail solo around the world.

✂ ┈┈┈✂┈┈┈┈┈

2 Discuss these questions with a partner.

1 Who do you know who is of a completely different mind-set to you? Do you get on well with this person?
2 What was the last mind-numbing experience you had?
3 Who do you know who is community-minded? What type of things do they do for the community?
4 What is the most mind-blowing experience you have ever had? What do you find mind-boggling?
5 What mindless things do you have to do in your everyday life?
6 Who do you know who is narrow-minded? single-minded? business-minded? absent-minded? In what way is this person like this?
7 Have you ever masterminded a plan? What was it? Was it successful?
8 What things are you mindful of in your everyday life?

Photocopiable

7A *Sentence halves*

José Miguel Galarza

Type of activity

Revision. Pair work.

Aim

To review and consolidate grammar and vocabulary from Units 1 to 6 of Inside Out Advanced Student's Book.

Task

To match sentence halves together.

Preparation

Make one copy of the worksheet for each pair of students. Cut up the cards as indicated.

Timing

20 minutes

Procedure

1 Divide the class into pairs and give each pair a set of cards. Ask the students to spread the cards face up on the table.

2 Explain that there are twelve sentences altogether and each card contains half of a sentence. Ask the students to match the halves together to make correct sentences.

3 Circulate and monitor, checking that the students have made the correct connections.

4 Check the answers with the whole class. (The sentences are correctly matched as they appear on the worksheet.)

Follow up

1 This exercise may well reveal some language areas that need reviewing. Be prepared to refer to the relevant units in the Inside Out Advanced Student's Book.

2 Ask the students, in pairs or small groups, to write some sentence halves of their own for another pair or group to match.

7A *Sentence halves*

The others caught up	with us an hour later.
The new job took a bit of getting	used to but I'm enjoying it now.
Gone are the days when	we had no responsibilities or worries.
There is little doubt	that she stole the money.
There are not believed	to be any survivors from the accident.
Under no circumstances	can we allow this to happen.
Only when I spoke to him	did I realise how little he knew about the situation.
If she had paid more attention at the time	she wouldn't be in such a mess now.
Not having a lot of time	they decided to take a taxi.
Woken by a strange noise	Harry decided to call the police.
Not only was she late for dinner	but she was also very rude to the host.
They finished their homework as	quickly as they could.

7B Early warning system

Piotrek Steinbrich

Type of activity

Reading and writing. Individual and pair work.

Aims

To practise writing skills.
To consolidate grammar from Units 1 to 6 of Inside Out Advanced Student's Book.

Task

To expand a short text.

Preparation

Make one copy of the worksheet for each pair of students. Cut up the cards as indicated.

Timing

40 minutes

Procedure

1   Divide the class into pairs and give each pair a copy of the *Early warning system* text. Allow them a few minutes to read it. Then explain any unfamiliar vocabulary.

2   Give each pair a set of cards. Explain that the students are going to expand the text using the words on the cards. As an example, read out a card and ask the students where they might put it in the text.

3   Working in pairs, ask the students to expand and rewrite the text. Circulate and monitor, helping as necessary.

4   When the students have finished, ask them to exchange their new texts with another pair to compare versions.

5   Invite several pairs to read their versions to the class.

Suggested answer

In a desert in Nevada, a few years ago, NASA was doing a test run for a future Mars expedition. **On the second day of the test**, a passing group of Native Americans, **who lived locally**, stopped to watch the **strange** goings-on. **Having some free time,** an **enthusiastic young** NASA official went over to talk to them. **Assuming they knew nothing of space travel**, he **carefully** explained that the work was in preparation for an expedition to explore Mars. The **mostly elderly** Native Americans **politely** asked if they could send a message for any life **that might be** on the planet. **Amused by the unusual request**, the NASA official **immediately** agreed. He took the message **they had written in their own language** back to the base headquarters. **Confused** NASA officials looked **repeatedly** at the message but, **not knowing the language**, none of them could understand it. **Several years later**, an expert on Native American languages came across the **forgotten** message and **when he translated it** burst out laughing. **It appeared that** the message read: "Watch out for these people – they come to take your land!"

7B *Early warning system*

Early Warning System

NASA was doing a test run for a future Mars expedition. A passing group of Native Americans stopped to watch the goings-on. A NASA official went over to talk to them. He explained that the work was in preparation for an expedition to explore Mars. The Native Americans asked if they could send a message for any life on the planet. The NASA official agreed. He took the message back to the base headquarters. NASA officials looked at the message but none of them could understand it. An expert on Native American languages came across the message and burst out laughing. The message read: "Watch out for these people – they come to take your land!"

a few years ago	amused by the unusual request	carefully	confused
elderly	enthusiastic	having some free time	that might be
strange	immediately	in a desert in Nevada	it appeared that
mostly	not knowing the language	on the second day of the test	forgotten
politely	repeatedly	Several years later	they had written in their own language
assuming they knew nothing of space travel	when he translated it	who lived locally	young

Photocopiable

7C *Phrasal verbs crossword*

Jon Hird

Type of activity

Vocabulary. Pair work.

Aim

To practise phrasal verbs.

Task

To complete a crossword with the verbs of phrasal verbs.

Preparation

Make one copy of the worksheet for each student.

Timing

20 minutes

Procedure

1 Divide the class into pairs and give each student a copy of the worksheet.
2 Ask the students, in pairs, to complete the crossword with the verbs of the phrasal verbs. Tell the students that they will need to put the verbs into appropriate tenses or forms.
3 When they have finished, ask each pair to compare their crosswords with another pair.
4 Check the answers with the whole class.

Answers

Across		**Down**	
4	flicked	1	slipped
6	butting	2	getting
8	came	3	drones
9	speak	5	catch
12	call	6	bottle
13	broken	7	tailed
14	talk	10	pick
16	look	11	bring
17	springing	14	thought
18	put	15	sort

7C *Phrasal verbs crossword*

Complete the crossword with the verbs of the phrasal verbs.

Across ▶

4 I didn't read it in detail. I just f_____ through it for a couple of minutes. (7)

6 He's always b_____ in when you're trying to have a conversation. It's so rude! (7)

8 The matter of your attendance c_____ up again in the meeting, I'm afraid. (4)

9 No-one will know how you feel if you don't s_____ up, will they? (5)

12 She isn't in the office at the moment. Could you c_____ back in about half an hour? (4)

13 Negotiations have b_____ down yet again. I'm not sure they'll ever find a solution. (6)

14 I think you should t_____ it through with them before you make a decision. (4)

16 I agree we need to get to the bottom of this. I'll l_____ into it straight away. (4)

17 These things do have a habit of s_____ up out of nowhere, don't they? (9)

18 I don't think I managed to p_____ across my ideas very well, I'm afraid. (3)

Down ▼

1 The office party was a bit boring so we s_____ off quietly. (7)

2 Working here is really g_____ me down at the moment. Maybe it's time to move on. (7)

3 He just d_____ on and on if you don't stop him. He loves the sound of his own voice. (6)

5 I missed a couple of days at work last week so I've got a lot of work to c_____ up with. (5)

6 You really shouldn't b_____ up your feelings so much. It would do you good to talk about it. (6)

7 His voice just t_____ off in disbelief when he saw the latest figures. (6)

10 We'll p_____ you up at your office at 6.30, OK? (4)

11 I think you should b_____ it up at the next meeting if you feel that strongly about it. (5)

14 Who t_____ up that idea? It's absolutely fantastic! (7)

15 We need to s_____ this mess out once and for all. (4)

Photocopiable

8A *Planet News*

Jon Hird

Type of activity

Reading and writing. Group work.

Aims

To practise summarising a text.
To practise using *will* for predictions.
To practise using the passive.

Tasks

To summarise newspaper articles.
To produce the front page of a newspaper of
the future.

Preparation

Make one copy of the worksheet for each student.

Timing

60–90 minutes

Procedure

1 Introduce the topic by asking the students to
think of the big news stories of this decade
(dotcom millionaires, mapping human genes,
cloning sheep, etc.). Then ask the students to
describe the breakthroughs predicted in the
next hundred years.

2 Divide the students into groups of three to
four students and give each student a copy of
the worksheet. Explain that the students are
not going to read the entire page. Ask them to
divide the page up so that each student reads
one or two articles each. Tell them to be
prepared to tell the rest of the group about
their articles. Circulate, helping with
vocabulary as necessary.

3 When they have finished, ask the students to
take turns to tell the rest of the group about
the articles they read.

4 Tell the students they are now going to
produce their own front page of a newspaper
of the future. Brainstorm a few ideas with the
whole class and then give the groups plenty
of time to come up with their own ideas, plan
their articles and decide who will write what.
Make sure all the students are involved in the
writing stage.

5 Ask the groups to write the articles and paste
them together to produce the front page of
their newspaper. Circulate and monitor,
helping with vocabulary as necessary.

6 When the groups have finished, display the
newspapers on the classroom wall. Allow the
students time to circulate and read the
other newspapers.

8A *Planet News*

www.planetnews.com

| News | Markets | Industries | Companies |

9 / 7 / 2 0 9 9   P L A N E T   N E W S

Earth meets its match

Yet further messages have been received from star 42 in the constellation Ursa Major. Messages from the newly-named 'Planet Eden' were first received last month by the Space Council's Planet Finder Mission and a team of the world's top scientists, linguists and computers have been analysing the recordings twenty-four hours a day since then. The messages are yet to be fully understood, but the Space Council's chief scientific officer, Marta Fernandez, said yesterday that patterns in the signals were beginning to emerge. She went on to say that even though the signals were originally transmitted thirty-five million years ago, this was absolute proof of the existence of extra-terrestrial, intelligent life. She described the discovery as the most exciting and important ever made. She added that as they'd sent messages to us, it was quite likely that they could also be on their way to visit.

The big sleep

Three men who 'died' thirty years ago were this morning having breakfast after being revived at midnight last night. Professor Scott Bowyer, who has headed the 'Eternal Life Project' since it began in 2069, announced the breakthrough this morning, saying that humans had at last conquered death. The three volunteers were frozen while they were still alive and have spent the last thirty years in capsules in Beijing University's cryogenics department. The three are currently undergoing a series of neuroscans and are having their mental and emotional states assessed. They will then have their brains uploaded with the major news and cultural stories of the past three decades.

150 years young

Vanessa Amilhat today became the first person to celebrate a 150th birthday. Born in Paris in 1949, she puts her longevity down to not worrying about money, walking a kilometre a day and a careful diet of vaccine and protein-enhanced food and drink. Madame Amilhat told reporters this morning that she didn't feel a day over a hundred and that she was looking forward to celebrating her 200th birthday in 2149.

From here to paternity

He's American, 1.85m tall, works out regularly at the gym and he's having a baby. David Venus, now seven months pregnant, was finally revealed to the world at the Earth Fertility Convention in New York yesterday. "I'm glad the sickness has stopped," Mr Venus told the conference while rubbing his swollen belly, adding "I'm feeling on top of the world and now I'm just looking forward to being a father."

First woman trillionaire

The publication of this year's 'World Rich List' has for the first time revealed more women than men among the world's hundred richest people. Dr Hillary Spencer, chief executive of GECL Industries, heads the list with an estimated worth of just over 2.2 trillion dollars. GECL, the world's largest company, employing over one million people worldwide, produces genetically engineered foods containing therapeutic proteins and vaccines and claims that if we eat carefully, we need never become ill again.

William Dawes, founder of EyeCom, which ten years ago developed the contact lens computer screen, is the world's richest man with an estimated fortune of 1.6 trillion dollars.

Others new to the list include Sam Smith, founder of NetSafe, the Internet security company, Linda Thomas, head of cosmetic laser-surgery company Biocos and Amber Arrows, pop singer, actress and politician.

Brazil crash out

In last night's World Premier Championship semi-finals, South-East Asia defeated Brazil by twelve goals to five and Saudi Arabia drew 4–4 with Scandinavia. Brazil's defeat means that Saudi Arabia are now favourites to win for the second year running.

Photocopiable

8B *Cyber quiz*

Jon Hird

Type of activity

Quiz. Individual and pair work.

Aims

To review language related to the Internet.
To discuss aspects of the Internet.

Task

To complete a quiz.

Preparation

Make one copy of the worksheet for each student.

Timing

20–30 minutes

Procedure

1 Introduce the topic by asking the students how much they know about the Internet. Ask them how often and why they use the Internet and if they have ever entered chat rooms.

2 Give each student a copy of the worksheet. Ask the students to work individually to complete the quiz. Circulate, helping with vocabulary as necessary.

3 When the students have finished, ask them to exchange worksheets with another student. Then check the answers with the whole class.

4 When everybody has been allocated a score, read out the analysis to the class. Hold a class feedback session. Did everybody agree with their analysis?

Answers

1 world wide web
2 c, a, b
3 c
4 b
5 b
6 b
7 a
8 b
9 c
10 c
11 **a** Are you OK? **b** thank you **c** great
d tomorrow **e** See you later
f Does anyone want to go?
12 **a** 2 **b** 4 **c** 1 **d** 3
13 (Students' own answers)

Analysis

How did you do?

Under 10
It really is time you woke up to the 21st century. Get someone to give you a few lessons before it's too late.

10–14
You've probably got a sensible balance between keeping up with cyber-technology and having a healthy existence away from your computer. You probably know as much as you need to know. Try to keep it this way.

Over 15
Well done, you certainly know your stuff, but don't forget, however, there is a whole world away from your computer screen, a world full of real people! Be careful!

8B Cyber quiz

Are you up-to-speed on computing and the Internet, or has cyber-technology passed you by? Do this quiz to find out.

1 What does *www* stand for? _____

2 Put the following into order of size, smallest to biggest.
  a 1MB **b** 1GB **c** 1KB

3 What do we call someone who illegally breaks into computer systems?
  a backer **b** tracker **c** hacker

4 What is an attachment?
  a extra hardware, e.g. scanner, printer, added to your computer system
  b a text or a picture added to an e-mail
  c a relationship made in a chat room

5 A website address is known as an URL. What does URL stand for?
  a Uncontrolled Random Looking
  b Uniform Resource Locator
  c Universal Reading List

6 Messages given to your computer by a website to enable quicker access on subsequent visits are known as:
  a biscuits **b** cookies **c** cakes

7 What is *Spam*?
  a junk e-mails
  b a computer language
  c an incompetent computer user (Stupid Person At Machine)

8 What is *snail mail*?
  a e-mails which take a long time to download
  b conventional post
  c e-mails which have been given a 'shell' to protect them from viruses

9 In a chat room, e-mail or telephone text message, typing in capital letters indicates the sender is:
  a also chatting/sending to someone else
  b not using their first language
  c angry or shouting

10 In a chat room or telephone text message, what does the message *BRB* mean?
  a Other people are reading our messages (Big Reader Base)
  b I need to get back to work (Boss Right Behind)
  c I need to go away for a short time (Be Right Back)

11 What do these abbreviations mean?
  (half point for each)
  a RU OK
  b TY
  c GR8
  d 2MORO
  e CU L8R
  f NE1 WAN2 GO?

12 'Smileys' are used to add emotion to messages. Match the smileys with their meaning.
  (half point for each)
  a xo)   **1** sad
  b x-(**2** bashful/shy
  c :-(**3** keep it quiet
  d :-x   **4** angry

13 Which of the following have you ever done?
  (half point for each)
  a used the internet
  b entered a chat room
  c arranged to meet someone in a chat room
  d sent an Internet greeting card
  e bought something online
  f set up your own website

8C Give us a clue

Russell Stannard

Type of activity

Speaking. Pair work.

Aim

To practise defining words related to computers and the Internet.

Task

To complete a crossword.

Preparation

Make one copy of the worksheet for each pair of students. Cut up the worksheet as indicated.

Timing

30–40 minutes

Procedure

1   Explain to the students that they are going to work in pairs to complete a crossword containing words related to computers and the Internet. Explain that each student in a pair has a half-completed crossword and they have to ask their partner for definitions to guess their missing clues. Do an example definition with the class, for example, *12 Down, It's connected to the keyboard of a computer and it moves the cursor on the computer screen (mouse).*

2   Divide the class into pairs, A and B, and give the students the appropriate half of the worksheet. Tell the students not to show each other their crosswords.

3   Allow the students time to prepare their definitions. Circulate, helping with vocabulary as necessary.

4   Students work in pairs to complete the crossword, asking and answering questions, for example,
    Student A: *What's 2 Down?*
    Student B: *It's the computer screen.*
    Student A: *Monitor?*
    Student B: *Yes, that's right. What's 5 Across?*

5   When most of the students have finished, check the answers with the whole class.

Answers

1D (Down) inbox: the part of your e-mail program where you find your new e-mails

2D monitor: the computer screen

3D surf: a verb to describe the way you explore the Internet

4D webcam: like a video camera but it broadcasts images over the Internet

5A (Across) scanner: converts images into digital form so that they can be stored or manipulated by computers

5D server: a central computer from which other computers obtain information

6A browser: the program that allows you to access the world wide web

7D graphics: drawings or artwork

8D hard drive: the part of your computer that holds all the information

9D software: a computer program and the instructions which control what a computer does

10D attachment: a file you add to an e-mail

11A programmer: the person who writes software for a computer

12A modem: a device that links a computer and a telephone so that data can be transmitted at high speeds from one computer to another

12D mouse: it's connected to the keyboard of a computer and it moves the cursor on the computer screen

13D keyboard: the set of keys on a computer that you press in order to make it work or type words

14A upgrade: to improve existing equipment

15D icon: a symbol on the computer screen, e.g. print, save, etc.

16A delete: to remove text, data, files, etc. from a computer

17A download: to transfer data from a large computer storage system to a smaller one

18A bookmark: to add a website address to the favourites menu so that you can access it again quickly

8C Give us a clue

A

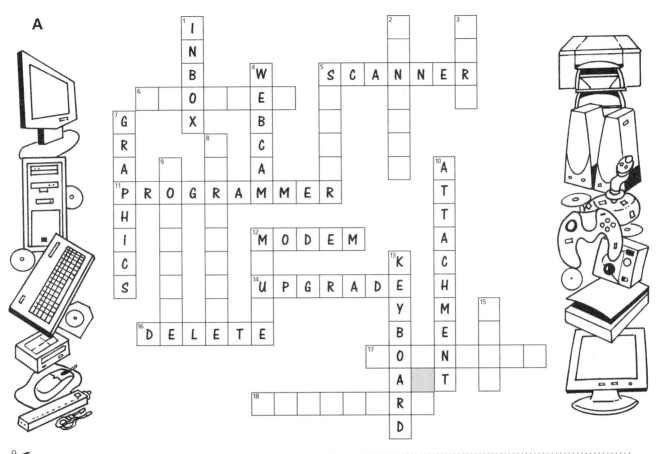

B

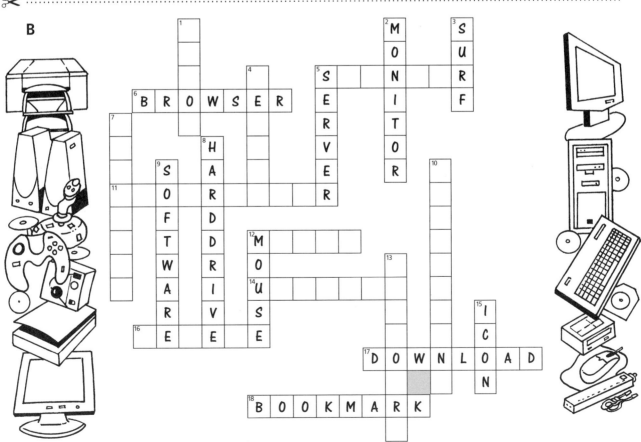

Photocopiable

9A Thick as thieves

Jon Hird

Type of activity

Reading and speaking. Pair work.

Aim

To practise speculating and making deductions.

Task

To speculate about or deduce from the context the information which is missing from incomplete stories.

Preparation

Make one copy of the worksheet for each pair of students.

Timing

30 minutes

Procedure

1 Explain that the students are going to read some true stories about failed robberies or about how robbers got caught. Explain that each story has a crucial piece of information missing. In most cases, the missing information is the action or event which resulted in their failures or in them getting caught.

2 Divide the class into pairs and give each pair a copy of the worksheet. Explain that the worksheet title *Thick as thieves* is an idiomatic expression which means to be very close or friendly, but in this case it is used as a play on words because the thief in each situation was thick (stupid).

3 Ask the students to read the stories and speculate about or deduce from the context what the missing information could be.

4 Conduct a class feedback session. Ask pairs to tell the class their ideas. Finish by confirming what the actual missing information was.

Answers

1 handed him over to the police
2 he put it in his pocket and set off the alarm as he left the store
3 four hundred police officers gathered for an official ceremony with Rio's governor
4 his business card fell unnoticed to the floor
5 that his wallet had been taken by a pickpocket while he was shopping
6 that the couple had unwittingly left their nine-month-old child behind
7 that he didn't have any money to pay for his ticket, and not wanting to make a fuss

9A *Thick as thieves*

In Linz in Austria, a nineteen-year-old youth held up a shop with an air rifle and took $200. A few days later, he saw a photofit picture in the local press and complained to his mother that it was a terrible likeness. She (1) *handed him over to the police* and he was immediately arrested.

In Camarillo, California, a man went into a department store and took several suits into a dressing room. He carefully snipped off the security tag from one suit and then put it on under his clothes. Rather than leave the security tag behind, thinking it would be found and used as evidence, (2) _____ _____ _____.

He was grabbed by a store employee as he stepped out of the store.

In January, a man was jailed for two years at Kingston Crown Court in England for the burglary of a flat three months before. He had left behind his wallet containing his passport. He insisted he was innocent of the crime claiming (5) _____ _____

earlier in the day.

After robbing bus passengers in Rio de Janeiro of more than $800 last month, the robber jumped off the bus right in front of (3) _____ _____ _____.

The commanding general of the military police himself abandoned the podium to give chase. The felon was eventually captured after a gun battle.

A couple and their sleeping baby shared a table with a Spanish tourist outside the Museum of Modern Art in New York. A few minutes after the couple left, the tourist realised that her handbag had been taken. The woman, noticing (6) _____ _____,

phoned the police and calmly waited for the thieves to return. They did indeed return ten minutes later and were promptly arrested.

A man entered the World Savings Bank in Plantation, Florida last month and demanded money. The teller said there were no envelopes to put the money in, so the robber pulled one from his pocket. As he did so, (4) _____ _____ _____.

The police telephoned him at work the next day and he was arrested five minutes later.

An armed robber was sentenced to eight years' imprisonment last week after being caught getting off a bus. The robber had attempted to hold up the Co-op Pioneer supermarket in Penzance, England, but fled empty-handed when told that the tills were empty. He ran out of the shop and straight onto a passing bus. Realising (7) _____ _____ _____ _____, he got off the bus and was arrested by the police.

Photocopiable

9B *The suspect*

Jenny Roden

Type of activity

Speaking and writing. Pair work.

Aim

To practise using fillers in conversation.

Task

To complete a dialogue.

Preparation

Make one copy of the worksheet for each student.

Timing

1–2 hours

Procedure

1 Introduce the topic by asking the students if they watch any TV police dramas and if so, which?

2 Explain that the students are going to complete a dialogue between a detective sergeant and a police constable. Make sure the students know the difference in rank. Divide the class into pairs and give each student a copy of the worksheet.

3 Ask the students to read the dialogue to get the gist. Make sure they understand who PC Brewer is (a police constable on a criminal observation), where he is (outside a suspect's house, in a police car) and how he is communicating (by mobile phone).

4 Ask the students, in their pairs, to complete the dialogue. Tell the students that they should consider the following when working through the dialogue:

   • using fillers, e.g. *The thing is ... | I'm afraid ...* (to show Brewer's embarrassment at having lost the suspect) and *Hang on | Just a second/minute,* etc. (to show that he's observing something).

   • using *But, ...* or *But, Sarge ...* (to show his indignation at being told off for going to buy chips).

   • using deductions, e.g. *(I think) he must have left. | It must be him!*

   • identifying when Brewer interrupts the sergeant.

   • giving a suitable description of Jimmy Slim, with some distinguishing feature, e.g. a limp or a scar.

5 When most students have finished, ask them to tell you their suggestions for PC Brewer's part.

6 Then ask the students, in their pairs, to practise reading their dialogue. Circulate, helping with pronunciation, stress and intonation, to show embarrassment, anger, indignation, excitement, etc.

7 Ask pairs to perform their dialogues for the class.

Suggested answers

a Evening, Sarge, Brewer here.

b Well ... er ... I'm afraid I've lost him.

c I think he must have left.

d Well, it must have been when I was getting some chips.

e But, Sarge! I'd been there for six hours and I was starving.

f And the chip shop's opposite the house.

g Shall I stick around till he comes back?

h I said, shall I stick around till he comes back?

i Hang on, there he is!

j I've just seen him.

k Oh yes, and he's talking to someone.

l (any description, but there must be some distinguishing feature)

m Just a minute ... Oh yes, he has.

n Hey, they're going off down the road now.

o Yes, Sarge.

Follow up

Ask the students to write, as a narrative, what happened before or afterwards.

9B *The suspect*

Complete the dialogue with appropriate words or phrases.

(Detective Sergeant Holmes is sitting at his desk. The phone rings.)

HOLMES: Holmes, here.

PC BREWER: a _____

HOLMES: Oh, yes, PC Brewer. How's the observation going?

PC BREWER: b _____

HOLMES: *(angrily)* What do you mean, you've lost him?

PC BREWER: c _____

HOLMES: You mean you didn't see him leave. How come?

PC BREWER: d _____

HOLMES: Getting some chips! I thought I told you not to take your eyes off the front door!

PC BREWER: e _____

HOLMES: Yes, I know you'd been there for six hours, but ...

PC BREWER: f _____

HOLMES: Yes, I know the chip shop's just opposite the house ...

PC BREWER: g _____

HOLMES: What?

PC BREWER: h _____

HOLMES: No, it's pointless waiting, he may not be back tonight.

PC BREWER: i _____

HOLMES: What's that ...

PC BREWER: j _____

HOLMES: Are you sure it's him?

PC BREWER: k _____

HOLMES: Can you describe the person he's talking to?

PC BREWER: l _____

HOLMES: It can't be true! This is better than we could ever have hoped for. It sounds like Jimmy Slim. Has he got an earring in his right ear?

PC BREWER: m _____

HOLMES: Then it must be him!

PC BREWER: n _____

HOLMES: Towards the canal you mean?

PC BREWER: o _____

HOLMES: Well, stay with them. Don't let them out of your sight. I'll send some back up. You lose him again Brewer and you'll be back on traffic duty, do you hear?

Photocopiable

10A *Notable seconds*

Jon Hird

Type of activity

Quiz. Team work.

Aim

To discuss answers to general knowledge
questions.

Task

To complete a general knowledge quiz.

Preparation

Make one copy of the worksheet for each team
of two to three students.

Timing

30 minutes

Procedure

1   Tell the students they are going to do a
    general knowledge quiz about people (or
    things) that have come second, not first.

2   Divide the class into small teams of two to
    three students and give each team a copy of
    the quiz.

3   Allow the students plenty of time to discuss
    the answers and complete the quiz. (Make
    sure they understand that the answer to the
    extra point section is not one of the
    alternatives given for the main question.)

4   When the teams have completed the quiz, ask
    them to exchange worksheets with another
    team. Then check the answers with the whole
    class. The team with the second highest score
    is the winner!

Answers

(Answers to extra point section in brackets.)

  1 a   (Mandarin Chinese)
  2 c   (Russian Federation)
  3 b   (Christianity)
  4 b   (Neil Armstrong)
  5 c   (London, Heathrow)
  6 b   (The letter *e*)
  7 c   (Finland)
  8 a   (spiders)
  9 b   (Nile)
10 c   (the)
11 a   (Ukraine)
12 a   (France)
13 b   (2nd Street)
14 b   (Tokyo)
15 c   (English)
16 c   (Mohammed)

Notes & comments

An alternative way of doing the quiz is to cut the
worksheet in half and give one half of the quiz to
one team and the other half to another team. Get
the teams to ask each other the questions and
record the answers given on the paper. The answers
are then marked and scores given. As before the
winner is the team with the second highest score.

10A *Notable seconds*

We all know lots of famous firsts, but what about those forgotten second places? Do this general knowledge quiz and find out how much you know about the world's runners-up. The team which has the second highest score is the winner!

1 Which is the second most spoken language in the world?

a English   **b** Arabic   **c** Spanish

For an extra point, which is the most spoken?

2 Which is the second biggest country in the world?

a the USA   **b** China   **c** Canada

For an extra point, which is the biggest?

3 Which religion has the second most followers?

a Buddhism   **b** Islam   **c** Hinduism

For an extra point, which religion has the most?

4 Who was the second man on the moon?

a Flash Gordon   **b** Buzz Aldrin   **c** Jim Lovell

For an extra point, who was the first?

5 Which is the world's second busiest airport?

a Tokyo (Narita)   **b** New York (JFK)   **c** Frankfurt

For an extra point, which is the world's busiest?

6 Which is the second most used letter in written English?

a s   **b** t   **c** o

For an extra point, which is the most used?

7 Which country drinks the second most coffee per person?

a Turkey   **b** Italy   **c** Sweden

For an extra point, which country drinks the most?

8 Which is the world's second most common phobia?

a flying   **b** the dark   **c** snakes

For an extra point, which is the most common?

9 Which is the second longest river in the world?

a Yangtze   **b** Amazon   **c** Mississippi

For an extra point, which is the longest?

10 Which is the second most spoken word in English?

a it   **b** you   **c** I

For an extra point, which is the most spoken?

11 Which is the second biggest country in Europe?

a France   **b** Spain   **c** Germany

For an extra point, which is the biggest?

12 Which is the second most visited country in the world?

a Spain   **b** the USA   **c** the UK

For an extra point, which is the most visited?

13 Which is the second most common street name in the USA?

a 1st Street   **b** 3rd Street   **c** 4th Street

For an extra point, what is the most common name?

14 Which is the second most populous city in the world?

a Mexico City   **b** Mumbai   **c** New York

For an extra point, which is the most populous?

15 Which is the second most used language on the Internet?

a French   **b** German   **c** Japanese

For an extra point, which is the most used?

16 What is the second most common name in the world?

a Ali   **b** José   **c** John

For an extra point, which is the most common?

Photocopiable

10B *Beating about the bush*

Piotrek Steinbrich

Type of activity

Speaking. Individual and group work.

Aim

To practise expressions from Unit 10 of Inside Out Advanced Student's Book.

Tasks

To explain the meaning of expressions.
To guess the expressions being described.

Preparation

Make one copy of the worksheet for each group of four students. Cut up the cards as indicated.

Timing

20 minutes

Procedure

1 Tell the students that they are going to test each other on some expressions that they learnt in Unit 10 of Inside Out Advanced Student's Book.

2 Divide the class into groups of four students and give each group a set of cards, placed face down on the table.

3 Ask each student in the group to take four cards. Tell the students not to show each other their cards. Ask the students to check what their expressions mean, if necessary, and be ready to explain the meaning, without using the words on the cards, to the rest of the group.

4 Ask the students to take it in turns to describe their expressions, remembering not to use the words on the cards. The others in the group guess the expressions.

5 Check the answers with the whole class.

10B *Beating about the bush*

mass production	first light
high profile	first lady
armchair rally driver	first-hand
once in a lifetime	first night
against the clock	first aid
precise details	from first to last
ardent fans	first language
multi-million	first and foremost

Photocopiable

10C *The queue*

Jenny Roden

Type of activity

Speaking. Group work. One-act play.

Aim

To practise pronunciation, stress and intonation.

Task

To perform a one-act play.

Preparation

Make one copy of the worksheet for each student.

Timing

1–2 hours

Procedure

1 Explain that students are going to perform a play about a queue. Introduce the topic by asking students to draw comparisons between ways of queuing (or not queuing!) in their countries. Elicit related vocabulary, e.g. *queue jumping, orderliness, pushing in front, jostling, keeping someone's place.*

2 Give a copy of the worksheet to each student and ask them to read it silently. Ask students their opinion of the play. Discuss any difficult vocabulary (*stand a chance, first come first served*) and the register which is used (fairly informal, with short sentences, contractions and ellipses). Point out that *mate* is mainly used between men as an informal term of address.

3 Divide the class into groups to practise reading the play aloud. Circulate, helping with pronunciation, stress and intonation. For example, practise the stress and intonation required to make A sound angry with *Hey! There's a queue you know!*

4 When each group has rehearsed the lines, ask them to rehearse standing up and moving, with actions and props. Given that the lines are short, encourage the students to learn their parts.

5 When everybody is ready, ask the groups to perform the play in turn, while the others are the audience.

Notes & comments

If you have a camcorder, the students might enjoy videoing each other's performances and watching themselves again.

10C *The queue*

(Several people are standing in a queue. It isn't possible to see the front of the queue, as it is obscured by a wall. B walks up)

B Excuse me, is this the queue for the free tickets?

A That's right, mate.

B Been waiting long?

A Not that long. About half an hour.

B Bit chilly, isn't it?

A Not bad for the time of year.

C *(Strolls up)* Excuse me, am I in the right place for the free tickets?

A That's right. Join the queue.

C Do you know how many tickets there are?

A About twenty I think.

B How did you hear about it?

A On the radio.

(D is passing by. He/She stops)

D What are you waiting for?

C The free tickets.

D Are they for tonight's show?

C I hope so. That's why I'm here.

D Are there a lot?

C Sounds like it.

(D joins the queue)

(E walks up to A, peers towards the front of the queue, then pushes in front of A)

A Hey, there's a queue you know!

E Sorry, are you waiting for the free tickets?

A Yeah, and been here a long time. The back of the queue's over there. *(Points)*

(E walks to the back)

C *(Taps B on the shoulder)* Excuse me, could I get you to keep my place? I'm going to get a hot dog. I won't be a moment.

(B nods. C walks off. D and E move up)

D I hope they get a move on. I'm getting cold.

E Do you know how many tickets there are?

D Not sure. Maybe around fifty.

(F and G, a couple, join the queue)

F I hope we get tickets. Do you think we stand a chance?

G I don't know. There are a lot of people here already.

E Excuse me, I couldn't help overhearing you. Actually, they say there are at least fifty.

F That's a relief. I'd hate to queue and find there are none left!

(C comes back from the hot dog stall. He walks up and down. He can't remember where he was in the queue. B waves)

B Over here, mate!

C Thank you. You haven't got very far. *(B shakes his head)*

(A mobile phone rings. Everyone one looks to see whose it is. It's A's)

A Oh, hi ... Yeah, I'm here now, in the queue. What? What do you mean? They can't do that! There's a lot of people going to be very disappointed. Yeah. Yeah. Right. *(He rings off and turns to B)* Looks like there are only going to be ten free tickets. My mate heard it on the radio.

C What's that?

D What did he say?

B Apparently there are only going to be ten free tickets.

E Only ten!

F That's dreadful! There are loads of people in front of us.

G Come on. What are we waiting for!

(G pushes his way along, past E, D, C, B and A pulling F with him by the hand. E looks put out but soon follows. D and C do the same. Finally B rushes after them and then A, shouting after them)

A Hey, you can't do that. It's first come, first served! I was here before you! Hey! Come back!

Photocopiable

11A *Letters that changed history*

Nicholas Sheard

Type of activity

Reading, speaking and writing. Pair and individual work.

Aim

To practise creative writing.

Task

To write a letter.

Preparation

Make one copy of the worksheet for each student.

Timing

45 minutes

Procedure

1 Give each student a copy of the worksheet and allow the students time to read the letters. Make sure that everybody knows what actually happened to these people.
a) American President Abraham Lincoln was shot dead at the theatre.
b) Bill Gates signed a deal with IBM but importantly retained exclusive rights to future upgrades and improvements. Because of this he was able to build his 'Microsoft' empire.
c) Prince Charles married Lady Diana Spencer in 1981. They divorced in the early 90s. Diana was killed in a car accident in Paris in 1998.
d) Paul McCartney met John Lennon at a church fair in Liverpool. Paul joined John's band and they eventually became 'The Beatles', the most famous and biggest-selling pop group of all time.

2 Divide the class into pairs and ask the students to discuss how these letters would have or might have changed the course of history had they in fact been sent, for example:
If Abraham Lincoln hadn't gone to the theatre, he wouldn't have been shot (that night).
If Bill Gates hadn't retained the rights, he probably wouldn't have been able to build such a dominant software empire.
If Prince Charles hadn't married Diana, he might have married Camilla Parker Bowles.
If John Lennon hadn't met Paul McCartney, the Beatles might never have existed.
Circulate and monitor, paying attention to correct use of past conditional forms and noting down errors for correction with the whole class. Then conduct a class feedback session to discuss the different possibilities.

3 Ask the students to discuss other ideas for more letters, for example, the head of the FBI writes to JFK and cancels his trip to Dallas. Brutus writes to Julius Caesar and tells him about the plot against him, etc. Ask the students to think of situations and write the letters that might have changed the course of history. Circulate as the students write, helping as necessary. Make sure the students use an appropriate style, formal or informal.

4 Display the letters on the classroom wall and allow the students time to read them. Then conduct a class feedback session. Ask the students to discuss how the letters would have changed the course of history if they had been sent.

11A *Letters that changed history*

Dear President Lincoln,

I regret to have to inform you that tonight's theatre performance has been cancelled. This is due to a last minute technical problem that cannot easily be remedied.

Please accept my sincere apologies for the inconvenience caused to you and your wife, and it is my sincere hope that we shall be able to reschedule the theatre visit in the near future.

Your humble servant,

Kurt N. Call

Kurt N. Call
Theatre Manager

Dear Diana

Thank you for your company the other night. I really enjoyed going to the theatre with you and hearing all about your work.

I'm writing because I'm sure you, like I, have been reading the newspapers and have seen the pictures of us together published in the tabloid press. I imagine that you have also read and heard people speculating about us, discussing the possibility that we may be having a relationship.

For this reason I feel that we shouldn't see each other again. I hope that this does not come as too much of a shock and that you understand. I would like to wish you every success for the future.

Charles

Dear Mr Gates,

Thank you for coming to visit us at IBM last week. We were very interested in the presentation you gave us of your new computer software (Microsoft), and, following preliminary trials, feel that you have a very good product.

IBM would be interested in using your 'Windows' software, but in agreeing to do so cannot agree to you retaining the rights to future upgrades and improvements.

We look forward to hearing how you wish to proceed.

Yours sincerely,

Jack Peachy

Jack Peachy

Dear Paul

It was good to meet you at the church fair last week. I'm glad that you enjoyed listening to my band and was pleased that you were interested in joining us.

Unfortunately I have had an argument with the other members of the band and we have split up. I hope you're not too disappointed about this. I want to be a painter, so I have decided to go to art college and won't have time for music any more. Good luck with everything.

Cheers

John

Photocopiable

11B *Easy money*

Russell Stannard

Type of activity

Reading and speaking. Pair work.

Aims

To practise reading for detail.
To practise retelling a story.

Tasks

To read and retell a story.
To discuss reasons why a story could be true
or false.

Preparation

Make one copy of the worksheet for each pair of
students. Cut up the worksheet as indicated.

Timing

30 minutes

Procedure

1 Divide the class into pairs, A and B, and give
each student the appropriate section of the
worksheet. Explain that one story on the
worksheet is true and the other is made up.
Tell the students not to show each other
their stories.

2 Ask the students to read their stories.
Circulate, helping with vocabulary
as necessary.

3 Then collect in the worksheets and ask the
students to retell their stories to their partner.

4 Now ask the students, in their pairs, to
discuss which story they think is true and
why. Encourage them to think of as many
reasons as they can for their choice.

5 Conduct a class feedback session. Invite pairs
to tell the class why they think Story A or B
is true. Have a class vote before you tell the
class that Story B is in fact the true story.

Notes & comments

At the time of publication the whole story could
be found on this website:
www.dnai.com/~pcombs/$$parti.html

11B *Easy money*

Story A

It was a normal Saturday morning. John Blake woke up, made some coffee and then sat down with the morning post. One particular letter caught his attention. It was addressed to him with 'urgent' printed on the front and looked rather official. He opened it. It read: *Dear Mr Blake, first BBTLotteries congratulate you and your family on your lottery success. The money has been deposited in your account and will be immediately available for withdrawal. You will be required to sign the enclosed forms and we would also like to advise you that our specialised financial advisors can help you to invest your money wisely and make a real success of your lottery winnings.*

John was confused. He had never played a lottery in his life. Questions were running through his head. How much money was involved? What had happened? What type of mistake was this? He quickly looked through all the other pieces of paper; among them was the one he had to sign. He began reading it through but his eyes were quickly attracted to a sentence in the corner. It read: *In receipt of $965,987 paid into City Central Bank, Boston, Account No. 34562 PY980.* He read it and read it again. This couldn't be true. Things like this just didn't happen in real life.

The next two days were the longest in John's life. On Monday morning he went into the City Central Bank in Boston and requested his credit situation. The teller took a piece of paper, wrote a number on a piece of paper and calmly handed it to John. It read: *The city bank would like to inform you that your current account is $1,009,000 in credit. Have a nice day.*

John left the money is his account for over six months. Then he took legal advice and had the money transferred into an off-shore account. It wasn't until the end of the financial year that BBTLotteries realised their mistake. The legal battle that took place lasted over two years.

- -

Story B

It was one of those stupid junk mails, you know, the promotional letters that you get sent to your house nearly every morning. You get them every day. *Patrick Combs, you have won $95,093.* There was a cheque for the same amount. The cheque was very real looking but in the corner was written 'non-negotiable for cash'. Patrick Combs read the rest of the advertisement. It told him that he could be earning real cheques just like this one if he did what they said. He looked at the cheque again. Real, he thought, this looks pretty real to me.

Of course he knew it was an advertisement but something in his head told him to try it. He thought it would make a funny story to tell his friends. Imagine saying 'Guess what! I put one of those advertising cheques in my bank account and the stupid bank passed it.'

So on the Monday morning on the way to work, he popped into his local bank and deposited the cheque. The teller never asked anything. She simply took the cheque, stamped it and gave him a receipt for the money. He wasn't that surprised. He knew that this didn't actually mean that he had been credited with the money. He knew that within three days he would receive a letter from the bank saying the cheque was invalid and hadn't been cleared.

Three days passed and no such letter arrived. A week later and still no letter. He went down to his nearest cash machine, popped in his card and requested his balance. The machine printed out on the screen: *Your balance is $104,889. Thank you for banking with Interstate Bank.*

He couldn't believe his eyes. It had been a joke. He had never expected them to accept the cheque, but even more he had never expected the cheque to come from a real account with real money in it. The cheque was an advertisement: how could they be so stupid to print a cheque that had a real bank account number on it?

The bank did eventually realise their mistake but by then Patrick Combs had already made plans to protect his money. The story went to national television, the Wall Street Journal and an amazingly complex legal battle with the bank in question.

Photocopiable

11C *Compound adjective dominoes*

Piotrek Steinbrich

Type of activity

Vocabulary. Group work.

Aim

To practise forming compound adjectives.

Task

To match dominoes to make compound adjectives.

Preparation

Make one copy of the worksheet for each group
of three to four students. Cut up the dominoes
as indicated.

Timing

20 minutes

Procedure

1 Explain that the students are going to play
a game of dominoes in which they form
compound adjectives.
2 Divide the class into groups of three to four
students and give each group a set of
dominoes placed face down on the table.
3 Ask the students to take five dominoes each
and leave the rest in a pile, face down.
4 Ask the students to take turns to place their
dominoes, for example,

If they do not have a domino that works, they
pick up a domino from the pile and miss a
turn. Circulate, checking that the students
have found the correct connections. The first
student to get rid of all their dominoes wins.

Notes & comments

To maximise oral practice, ask the students to say
each word as they play.

11C *Compound adjective dominoes*

lost	empty-	handed	well-
dressed	broken-	hearted	open-
minded	home-	made	long-
winded	right-	handed	well-
behaved	cold-	hearted	absent-
minded	ready-	made	long-
suffering	single-	handed	well-
informed	faint-	hearted	bloody-
minded	man-	made	long-
running	heavy-	handed	well-
fed	warm-	hearted	like-
minded	self-	made	long-

Photocopiable

12A *British and American English*

Jenny Roden

Type of activity

Writing. Pair work.

Aim

To practise American English words.

Task

To complete a crossword with American English words.

Preparation

Make one copy of the worksheet for each student.

Timing

20–40 minutes

Procedure

1 Divide the class into pairs and give each pair a copy of the worksheet.

2 Ask the students to complete the crossword with the American English equivalent of the British English words in the clues.

3 Then ask pairs to to compare their answers with another pair.

4 Check the answers with the whole class.

Answers

Across		Down	
1	garbage	**2**	elevator
3	semester	**4**	subway
5	store	**6**	closet
6	cab	**9**	diapers
7	downtown	**10**	freeway
8	yard	**11**	smart
10	fall	**12**	sidewalk
14	automobile	**13**	faucet
15	purse		
16	pants		
17	jelly		

Follow up

1 Ask the students to tell the class any other American English words or expressions that they know.

2 Ask the students to make a list of another ten American English words or expressions for homework.

12A British and American English

Complete the crossword with the American English equivalent of the British English words.

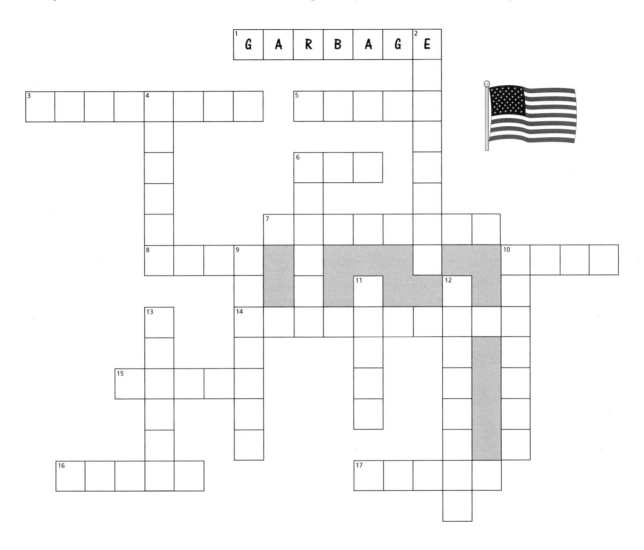

Across ▶

1 rubbish (7)
3 (college) term (8)
5 shop (5)
6 taxi (3)
7 town centre (8)
8 garden (4)
10 autumn (4)
14 car (10)
15 handbag (5)
16 trousers (5)
17 jam (5)

Down ▼

2 lift (8)
4 underground (tube) (6)
6 wardrobe (6)
9 nappies (7)
10 motorway (7)
11 clever (5)
12 pavement (8)
13 tap (6)

Photocopiable

12B *Ode to the spell checker*

Jon Hird

Type of activity

Reading and writing. Pair work.

Aim

To identify homophones and correct the spellings.

Task

To rewrite a poem with the correct spellings.

Preparation

Make one copy of the worksheet for each pair of students.

Timing

20 minutes

Procedure

1 Read the poem aloud to the students and elicit from them what it is about. (It's a poem about a computer spell checker, a supposedly reliable resource for locating spelling errors in a document.) Explain the meaning of any unfamiliar words.

2 Divide the class into pairs and give each pair a copy of the worksheet. Ask the students to read the poem and to say why it contains so many incorrect spellings. Then ask them to rewrite the poem with the correct spellings. Circulate and monitor, helping as necessary.

3 When they have finished, ask pairs to compare their answers with another pair.

4 Check the answers with the whole class. Either invite individual students to write a line of the poem on the board, or hand out a photocopy of the correct version of the poem.

Answers

I have a spelling checker
It came with my PC
It clearly marks for my review
Mistakes I cannot see.

I strike a key and type a word
And wait for it to say
Whether I am wrong or I am right
It shows me straight away.

As soon as a mistake is made
It knows before too long
And I can put the error right
It's rarely ever wrong.

I have run this poem through it
I am sure you're pleased to know
It's letter perfect all the way
My checker told me so.

12B Ode to the spell checker

Rewrite the poem with the correct spellings.

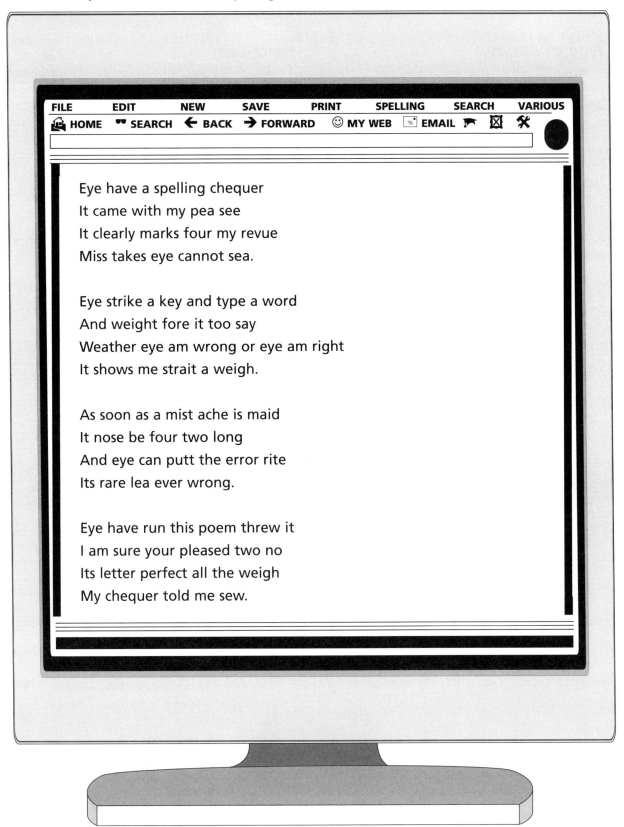

FILE   EDIT   NEW   SAVE   PRINT   SPELLING   SEARCH   VARIOUS

🏠 HOME   ⭐ SEARCH   ← BACK   → FORWARD   ☺ MY WEB   ✉ EMAIL   ⌖   ⌧   ✖

Eye have a spelling chequer
It came with my pea see
It clearly marks four my revue
Miss takes eye cannot sea.

Eye strike a key and type a word
And weight fore it too say
Weather eye am wrong or eye am right
It shows me strait a weigh.

As soon as a mist ache is maid
It nose be four two long
And eye can putt the error rite
Its rare lea ever wrong.

Eye have run this poem threw it
I am sure your pleased two no
Its letter perfect all the weigh
My chequer told me sew.

   Photocopiable

12C *Word jigsaw*

Nicholas Sheard

Type of activity

Revision. Group work.

Aim

To revise vocabulary and grammar by constructing sentences.

Task

To construct sentences containing words collected from a board game.

Preparation

Make one copy of the worksheet (enlarged to A3 size if possible) for each group of four students. You will need one dice per group and one counter per student.

Timing

40 minutes

Procedure

1 Divide the class into groups of four students and give each group a copy of the worksheet.

2 Explain that the aim of the game is to collect as many points as possible by making grammatically correct sentences.

3 Look at the board game with the class. Explain the rules:

- Students take turns to throw the dice and move round the board. When they land on a square they choose one of the words in the square and write it down in their notebooks. Students then cross out the word they chose on the board so that it cannot be used again.

- Each time a student passes 'Go', he/she has to write a sentence containing the words he/she collected going round the board that time. (Verb forms can be changed, e.g. *be* can be changed to *being, is, are, was, were, been* and nouns can be singular or plural.) Students read out their sentences and the rest of the group adds up their score. Students score one point for each word used and lose one point for each word not used. Circulate and monitor, making notes of any errors to correct at the end.

- Students each go round the board twice and they cannot use any of the words they or anybody else in the group have already crossed out. (As the game progresses, students will find that squares have no available words.)

4 At the end of the game the winner is the player with the most points.

5 Conduct a class feedback session. Invite individual students to read out some of their sentences.

Notes & comments

As in all games there is an element of luck, which makes it fun and addictive. This game is a flexible resource that can be adapted to suit all levels by erasing the words given and writing in others.

12C *Word jigsaw*

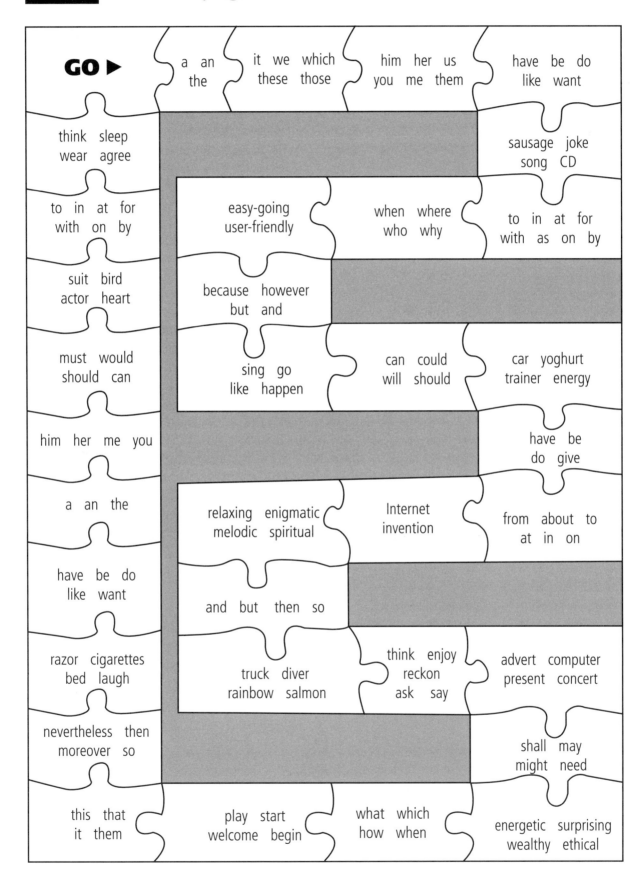

GO ▶

a an the

it we which these those

him her us you me them

have be do like want

think sleep wear agree

sausage joke song CD

to in at for with on by

easy-going user-friendly

when where who why

to in at for with as on by

suit bird actor heart

because however but and

must would should can

sing go like happen

can could will should

car yoghurt trainer energy

him her me you

have be do give

a an the

relaxing enigmatic melodic spiritual

Internet invention

from about to at in on

have be do like want

and but then so

razor cigarettes bed laugh

truck diver rainbow salmon

think enjoy reckon ask say

advert computer present concert

nevertheless then moreover so

shall may might need

this that it them

play start welcome begin

what which how when

energetic surprising wealthy ethical

13A *Pink dolphins*

Nicholas Sheard

Type of activity

Reading. Pair and group work.

Aim

To practise taking part in a meeting.

Task

To play a role in a discussion about ethical tourism and development.

Preparation

Make one copy of the worksheet for each student.

Timing

60 minutes

Procedure

1 Introduce the topic by asking the students to think of any natural unspoilt beauty spots in their country. Does the tourist industry in their country protect or alter these natural beauty spots for commercial or other purposes? How do the students feel about this?

2 Before reading the text, find out how many students in the class would like to go to the Amazon rainforest on holiday. Give each student a copy of the worksheet and allow them five minutes to read the article. In pairs or small groups, ask the students to discuss whether they have changed their minds after reading the text.

3 Ask the students to read the information about developing tourism at Lake Tarapoto and the instructions for the task. Check that the students understand what they have to do. Divide the class into groups of five and assign a role to each student.

4 Allow the students time to prepare their arguments. Circulate and monitor, helping with vocabulary as necessary.

5 Ask the students to hold a meeting in their groups to discuss the issue. Before starting their meetings, ask each group to nominate a chairperson and a person to take the minutes. Set a fifteen-minute time limit for the meetings.

6 Allow the groups another five minutes to discuss and finalise the minutes.

7 Ask each group to present their decisions to the class. Hold a class discussion on the outcomes.

13A *Pink dolphins*

Hidden deep within the Amazon rainforest in the south of Colombia is Lake Tarapoto, home to a rare and almost mythical species: Inia geoffrensis or pink river dolphin. Thought by some to be extinct, this fresh-water dolphin had simply been forgotten and in 1987 a Colombian biologist, Fernando Trujillo, made it his life mission to study and protect them.

It wasn't easy for him. Not only had he to understand the local Indian culture, but he also had to deal with a corrupt local bureaucracy, a far from eco-friendly fishing lobby and the vested interests of the logging and industrial sectors, which were busy polluting the river close to the lake. And then there was the rainforest itself, where the delicately balanced ecosystem is at odds with every aspect of the modern world.

Trujillo began a study of flowers growing near the lake after he heard an old myth that fish are created from the falling petals of a magical tree. It was an enchanting explanation for what turned out to be a biological truth. Many of the fish in the lake relied upon these petals for food. Any deforestation would therefore help to deplete an important source of food for the fish.

Trujillo has come to see the dolphins as part of the wider, carefully balanced ecosystem and has encouraged the local Ticuna tribe to rediscover traditional fishing methods. The use of spears for fishing might not be as effective in the short-term as nets, but they are preferable when fish stocks have been reduced to a non-sustainable level. It has been revealed that, until recently, nearly thirty dolphins died every year after being caught in fishermen's nets. Now the number of deaths is down to two or three a year.

As a means of boosting the local economy, the Colombian government is considering developing tourism at Lake Tarapoto. As well as those from the business world who are in favour of such a development, there is some resistance from the local community, who feel that this place of natural beauty could be irreparably damaged.

In groups of five, each choose a role-card for a debate. Read your role-card and make notes on what you are going to say. Be prepared to state your case either for or against the development and be able to justify your reasons. Then, in your group, hold a meeting to discuss the plan.

Local Ticuna Indian	**Local government official**
You are concerned that your peaceful village life close to the lake will be adversely affected by the arrival of tourists. This feeling is shared by most of the local community. On the other hand, you believe that your knowledge of the area might enable you to get a job as a tour guide. You want assurances that, should development go ahead, tourist numbers will be restricted and for only two months of the year.	You feel that promoting tourism at Lake Tarapoto would be a good way to generate much-needed money for the local community. You are insistent that the profits generated from any tourist activity should be used locally to improve the standard of living of local people and not go into the pockets of a few business entrepreneurs. You want a long-term, sustainable and equitable solution to tourist development in the area.
Fernando Trujillo	**Business entrepreneur**
You are against turning Lake Tarapoto into a tourist resort. You are concerned that the natural habitat of many species, including that of the pink river dolphin, will be irreparably damaged and that the delicately balanced ecosystems will be ruined for ever. You want the lake and its environs to be given special protected status and for there to be no development whatsoever. You have the backing of most of the local community.	You are desperate to turn Lake Tarapoto into a tourist attraction and are seeking permission to build a hotel, close to the lake. You have future plans to develop even more hotels and associated facilities. You would also like local transportation to be improved to ease access to the resort. This would mean cutting through the rainforest to build a new road. You would also like boat trips to be made available to tourists at the resort.

Independent advisor to the government
You are truly independent on this issue. You must listen to all the participants, asking questions as necessary and finally make a decision whether or not to proceed with the development.

Photocopiable

13B *Spare change*

Jenny Roden

Type of activity

Speaking. Pair and group work. One-act play.

Aim

To practise pronunciation, stress and intonation.

Task

To perform a one-act play.

Preparation

Make one copy of the worksheet for each student.

Timing

1–2 hours

Procedure

1 Write *Spare change* on the board and elicit from the students what this means. Ask the students if they ever give money to people begging in the street. If they do, ask them how they choose who to give to (e.g. young or old people, mothers with babies, the disabled, buskers, etc.) and how much to give. Do they give more to people who entertain rather than simply beg?

2 Give each student a copy of the worksheet and ask them to read it silently. Ask the students their opinion of the play. Do they feel sympathetic towards A? Explain the meaning of any unfamiliar words.

3 Divide the class into pairs to read parts A and B aloud. Circulate as the students are reading and help with pronunciation, stress and intonation. For example, practise the stress and intonation required to make A sound surprised (*What d'you mean?*) or cynical (*That's about all I've got!*).

4 When the students have rehearsed the lines in pairs, ask them to form groups of six to eight students and rehearse the play again, taking it in turns to play parts A and B. Encourage them to make a sign and find a collecting box, some loose change and a coat and hat.

5 When everybody is ready, ask the groups to perform the play in turn, while the others are the audience. If you have a camcorder, the students might enjoy videoing each other's performances and watching themselves again.

Follow up

Invite some students to perform the play without the script. They do not have to get the lines exactly right.

Notes & comments

The play has only two proper speaking parts, so initially it should be rehearsed in pairs. Then divide the students into groups of six to eight. Although students can, of course, choose their parts, A is technically a part for a male, while B and C could be male or female.

13B *Spare change*

(A is sitting on a bench with a sign that reads 'hungry and homeless' propped up beside him. There's a collecting box in front of him and he's wearing a suit. In contrast, C is sitting a little further on, dressed in shabby, dirty clothes, the coat tied up with string and using a hat for collecting. Almost every passer-by puts money in C's hat. C acknowledges the donations with 'Thank you, sir/ma'am. God bless you, sir/ma'am.' This continues in the background all the time that A and B are conversing. None of the passers-by put money in A's box)

A Spare change? Can you spare any change for a cup of tea?

(Passer-by stares and walks on)

A Spare change? Can you spare any change for a cup of tea?

(Another passer-by stares and walks on)

A Could you spare any change, sir?

(B stops. Puts money in the collecting box and walks on)

A Thank you, sir!

(B pauses and walks back)

B I hope you don't mind my asking, but are you really hungry and homeless?

A Yes, just what the sign says. *(He motions to his sign)*

B It's just that you don't look as if you are.

A What d'you mean?

B You're too smart.

A Smart?

B Yes, tramps, *(Corrects himself)* ... I mean, people in your situation don't usually wear a suit.

A I see what you mean, but the truth is, it's the only decent thing I've got left. I've lost my job and been evicted from my house. I had to sell everything. I used to work on the buses, but there's no call for bus conductors nowadays.

B I see. *(Moves off, pauses and comes back)* Well, I don't mean to be rude, but it'd make a lot of sense to sell your suit, if you need the money. That's a nice suit you've got there.

A Believe me, the thought has crossed my mind, but I've got my dignity you know ... although that's about all I've got! *(Laughs sarcastically)* Besides, I need it to look for a job.

B Isn't it difficult to apply for a job when you haven't got an address?

A Ah, but that's where you're wrong! I have. It's here! *(Points to the bench)* 'The Bench, Queens Park, Queen's Square.' It's even got its own postcode. Didn't you read about it in the papers? It's a new experiment by the council to help homeless people like me find jobs.

B That sounds like a good idea. But, if you're not going to look the part, so to speak, why don't you do something?

A Do something?

B Yes, you know, do some busking, read poems, or stand still like a statue. *(He poses)*

A I would if I could, but I can't. I'm not very artistic. If only I were!

B *(Shrugs his shoulders)* Oh, well, I must be going. It was nice talking to you. Here, take this and buy yourself a meal. *(Hands A a five-pound note)*

A Much obliged, sir!

(People continue to walk by. Some ignore A, some stare, none give anything. Finally A gives up, picks up his sign and box and leaves. A few more people pass by and throw money into C's hat)

14A *You bet!*

Ruth Sánchez García

Type of activity

Writing. Pair work.

Aim

To review and consolidate grammar and vocabulary from Units 8 to 13 of Inside Out Advanced Student's Book.

Task

To correct the errors in fifteen sentences and to bet according to how confident the students are about their corrections.

Preparation

Make one copy of the worksheet for each pair of students.

Timing

30–40 minutes

Procedure

1   Divide the class into pairs and give each pair a copy of the worksheet.

2   Tell the students that each sentence contains a grammatical or vocabulary error. Ask them to work in their pairs to identify and correct the mistakes.

3   When the pairs have finished, ask them to bet on each sentence according to how confident they are that they have successfully corrected it. The more confident the students are, the more they should bet. Give each pair an imaginary total of £100 and tell them the maximum bet per sentence is £10 and the minimum £1. Ask the students to write the amount they'd like to bet for each sentence in the box. Tell them to make sure the total amount they bet does not exceed £100.

4   Check the answers with the whole class (or ask pairs to exchange worksheets for correction). For each successfully corrected sentence, the pair wins the amount they bet. If the sentence was not successfully corrected, the money is lost.

5   The pair with the most money is the winner.

Answers

1   We've got a very good chance of getting there in time if we leave now.

2   They probably won't have arrived until midnight at the earliest.

3   She didn't want to go and neither did we to be honest.

4   Well, it didn't really live up to our expectations.

5   It can't have been him – he wasn't here at the time.

6   Given the choice, I'd rather go to the Caribbean.

7   I finally got him to take me to Paris for the weekend.

8   First and foremost, I'd like to thank everyone for coming.

9   I think it's against the law here.

10 It really is a once in a lifetime opportunity.

11 We looked everywhere, but we couldn't find it, I'm afraid.

12 Not only did he lose his bag, but all his money as well.

13 We were on the verge of giving up hope when we found it.

14 I won't tell anyone at all. You have my word.

15 It really is time we left – come on or we'll be late.

Notes & comments

The activity can also be done as a simple error correction activity without the betting. Ask the students to make the corrections and then check the answers with the whole class.

14A *You bet!*

B E T

1   We've got a very good chance to get there in time if we leave now.

2   They won't probably have arrived until midnight at the earliest.

3   She didn't want to go and neither we did to be honest.

4   Well, it didn't really live to our expectations.

5   It mustn't have been him – he wasn't here at the time.

6   Given the choice, I'd go rather to the Caribbean.

7   I finally got him take me to Paris for the weekend.

8   Foremost and first, I'd like to thank everyone for coming.

9   I think it's against law here.

10   It really is a one in a lifetime opportunity.

11   We looked everywhere, but we couldn't have found it, I'm afraid.

12   Not only he lost his bag, but all his money as well.

13   We were on the verge to give up hope when we found it.

14   I won't tell anyone at all. You have my words.

15   It really is time we leave – come on or we'll be late.

14A *You bet!*

Photocopiable

14B *Tell us about ...*

Jon Hird

Type of activity

Speaking and listening. Group work.

Aim

To improve fluency.

Task

To move around a board by speaking about different topics for sixty seconds at a time.

Preparation

Make one copy of the worksheet for each group of three to four students. Each group needs one dice and a watch with a second hand and each student needs a counter.

Timing

30 minutes

Procedure

1 Divide the class into groups of three to four students and give each group a copy of the worksheet.

2 Look at the board game with the class and explain how to play:
   - Each student places his/her counter anywhere on the board.
   - Students take turns to throw the dice, move the appropriate number of squares, read the prompt in the square and talk continuously about that topic for one minute.
   - If a player lands on a *Tell us about ...* square, the other students in the group choose a topic for him/her to talk about.
   - If a student manages to talk for sixty seconds, he/she gets a point. However, if the student hesitates too often, repeats information or does not manage to talk for the full sixty seconds, he/she does not get a point.
   - The winner in each group is the first student to get five points.

3 While the students are playing the game, circulate and monitor, noting down any common errors which can be used for correction at a later stage.

Follow up

Prepare a *Correct the mistake* activity using the errors that you noted down while the students were playing.

14B *Tell us about ...*

My favourite gadget is ...	By the end of the year, I'll have ...	In the third millennium, we ...	If I could no longer use a computer, ...	**Tell us about ...**
Tell us about ...				I've never been able to ...
I often feel guilty about ...				My favourite computer game is ...
It's high time I ...	A charity I support is ...		The worst crimes are ...	I generally use the Internet to ...
	Some English words used in my language are ...		It's OK to break the law if ...	
The last letter I wrote in English ...	**Tell us about ...**		**Tell us about ...**	My country's press is ...
A traditional story from my country is ...				I'll never forget the first time I ...
A story I remember from my childhood is ...	I once won ...	**Tell us about ...**	The main differences between my first language and English are ...	It's always been an ambition of mine to ...

Photocopiable

14C *Pair or pear?*

Ruth Sánchez García

Type of activity

Vocabulary and pronunciation. Pair work.

Aim

To practise homophones.

Tasks

To match words to their definitions.
To find words from their pronunciation
and definition.

Preparation

Make one copy of the worksheet for each pair of
students. Provide monolingual dictionaries.

Timing

20 minutes

Procedure

1   Introduce the topic of homophones by asking
    the students to give some examples of words
    that sound the same but are spelt differently,
    e.g. *right/write, fare/fair*, etc.
2   Divide the class into pairs and give each pair
    a copy of the worksheet. Explain that there
    are ten pairs of definitions, and that each
    word in the box corresponds to one of the
    definitions in each pair. Explain that this
    word has a homophone that corresponds to
    the other definition in each pair.
3   Ask the students to match each word in the
    box to its definition, then match that word
    to its phonetic script in the border.
4   Then ask the students to work out the
    homophone that corresponds to the other
    definition in each pair. Circulate, helping
    as necessary.
5   When all the pairs have finished, check the
    answers with the whole class.

Answers

1   J   pair, pear
2   C   medal, meddle
3   A   whole, hole
4   E   sighs, size
5   G   seller, cellar
6   I   mail, male
7   F   tyre, tire
8   H   hair, hare
9   B   heard, herd
10   D   serial, cereal

Follow up

Ask the students to think of more homophones,
e.g. *bare/bear, pour/paw, queue/cue, heir/air*, etc.

14C *Pair or pear?*

Ⓐ /həʊl/   **Ⓑ** /hɜːd/

Ⓒ /ˈmedl/

Ⓘ /peə/

Ⓓ /ˈsɪəriəl/

Ⓙ /meɪl/

Ⓔ /saɪz/

Ⓗ /heər/

Ⓖ /ˈselə/

Ⓕ /ˈtaɪə/

Read the pairs of definitions for homophones 1–10. Match each word in the box to one definition in each pair. Then match the phonetic scripts (A–J) to each pair. Then write the other word in each pair. Use a dictionary if necessary.

> cellar   hair   heard   mail   medal   serial   pear   tyre   sighs   whole

1 ☐   **a** a couple _____
           b a fruit with yellow or green skin and white flesh *pear*

2 ☐   **a** a flat piece of metal given as a prize for bravery or in sports _____
           b to interfere _____

3 ☐   **a** all of something _____
           b an opening, cavity or hollow space in something _____

4 ☐   **a** deep breaths _____
           b how big something or someone is _____

5 ☐   **a** a person or business that sells things _____
           b a room used to store things _____

6 ☐   **a** what the postman delivers _____
           b belonging to the sex which does not have babies or lay eggs _____

7 ☐   **a** part of the wheel of a car _____
           b to feel that you need to rest or sleep _____

8 ☐   **a** found on your head (unless you're bald!) _____
           b a very fast animal similar to a rabbit _____

9 ☐   **a** the past tense of *hear* _____
           b a group of the same kind of animal that live together _____

10 ☐   **a** a story that is told in a number of parts _____
           b a popular breakfast food, served with milk _____

Photocopiable